Cambridge Elements

Elements in Political Economy
edited by
Mark Dincecco
University of Michigan

THE POLITICAL ECONOMY OF CHINA'S IMPERIAL EXAMINATION SYSTEM

Erik H. Wang
New York University

Clair Z. Yang
University of Washington

Shaftesbury Road, Cambridge CB2 8EA, United Kingdom

One Liberty Plaza, 20th Floor, New York, NY 10006, USA

477 Williamstown Road, Port Melbourne, VIC 3207, Australia

314–321, 3rd Floor, Plot 3, Splendor Forum, Jasola District Centre,
New Delhi – 110025, India

103 Penang Road, #05–06/07, Visioncrest Commercial, Singapore 238467

Cambridge University Press is part of Cambridge University Press & Assessment,
a department of the University of Cambridge.

We share the University's mission to contribute to society through the pursuit of
education, learning and research at the highest international levels of excellence.

www.cambridge.org
Information on this title: www.cambridge.org/9781009663298

DOI: 10.1017/9781009347600

© Erik H. Wang and Clair Z. Yang 2025

This publication is in copyright. Subject to statutory exception and to the provisions of relevant collective licensing agreements, with the exception of the Creative Commons version the link for which is provided below, no reproduction of any part may take place without the written permission of Cambridge University Press & Assessment.

An online version of this work is published at doi.org/10.1017/9781009347600 under a Creative Commons Open Access license CC-BY-NC 4.0 which permits re-use, distribution and reproduction in any medium for non-commercial purposes providing appropriate credit to the original work is given and any changes made are indicated. To view a copy of this license visit https://creativecommons.org/licenses/by-nc/4.0

When citing this work, please include a reference to the DOI 10.1017/9781009347600

First published 2025

A catalogue record for this publication is available from the British Library

ISBN 978-1-009-66329-8 Hardback
ISBN 978-1-009-34761-7 Paperback
ISSN 2398-4031 (online)
ISSN 2514-3816 (print)

Additional resources for this publication at www.cambridge.org/ErikHwang

Cambridge University Press & Assessment has no responsibility for the persistence or accuracy of URLs for external or third-party internet websites referred to in this publication and does not guarantee that any content on such websites is, or will remain, accurate or appropriate.

For EU product safety concerns, contact us at Calle de José Abascal, 56, 1°, 28003 Madrid, Spain, or email eugpsr@cambridge.org

The Political Economy of China's Imperial Examination System

Elements in Political Economy

DOI: 10.1017/9781009347600
First published online: May 2025

Erik H. Wang
New York University

Clair Z. Yang
University of Washington

Author for correspondence: Erik H. Wang, erik.wang@nyu.edu

Abstract: Just as councils and assemblies were central to European polities for centuries, the imperial examination system (*Keju*) constituted the cornerstone of state institutions in China. This Element argues that *Keju* contributed to political stability, and its emergence was a process, not a shock, with consequences initially unanticipated by its contemporaries. The Element documents the emergence of *Keju* using evidence from early Chinese empires to the end of the Tang Dynasty in the 10th century, including epitaphs and government documents. It then traces the selection criteria of *Keju* and trends in social mobility over the second millennium, leveraging biographical information from over 70,000 examinees and 1,500 ministers and their descendants. The Element uses a panel of 112 historical polities to quantify *Keju*'s association with country-level political indicators against the backdrop of global convergence in political stability and divergence in institutions. This title is also available as Open Access on Cambridge Core.

Keywords: political economy, institutions, Chinese imperial examination system (*Keju*), Great Divergence, Chinese history

© Erik H. Wang and Clair Z. Yang 2025

ISBNs: 9781009663298 (HB), 9781009347617 (PB), 9781009347600 (OC)
ISSNs: 2398-4031 (online), 2514-3816 (print)

Contents

1	Introduction	1
2	The Origins	5
3	Early Development	23
4	Evolution of *Keju* over Time	43
5	*Keju* and Political Stability	63
	References	74

1 Introduction

The "Great Divergence," in which Western Europe industrially outpaced the rest of the world by the early 19th century, has puzzled scholars for centuries. Recent studies tracing its origins increasingly point to a deeper, underlying *political* divergence that may have begun much earlier (Cox, 2017; Dincecco and Wang, 2018; Stasavage, 2020; Huang and Yang, 2022; Fernández-Villaverde et al., 2023; Chen, Wang, and Zhang, 2025). Central to this political divergence is the role of institutions, such as European parliaments. These parliaments limited the power of rulers through checks and balances, while the resulting credible commitments fostered political stability to a degree far greater than what was seen in many other parts of the world (Blaydes and Chaney, 2013).

We argue in this Element that an important parallel institutional development in East Asia was the Imperial Civil Service Examination System, hereafter referred to as *Keju* (科举). *Keju* served as a method of recruiting officials for the imperial government through a standardized written test on Confucian classics and literature – a test that was open to most males. Emerging sometime between 587 and 622 CE and lasting until 1905 CE, *Keju* was not only an outcome of political development but also a potential contributor to the political divergence that set the East and West on different historical paths. Crucially, *Keju* enabled Chinese monarchs to maintain political stability comparable to that of their European counterparts, without the need for concessions resembling parliamentary constraints (Figure 13 and Table 2).

1.1 Twin Arguments

This Element makes two arguments regarding the link between *Keju* and long-run political development.

Argument 1

Keju contributed to stability and the consolidation of absolutism by fulfilling a political function. By evaluating candidates based on exam performance rather than family background or social status, and with its inclusiveness toward most males, *Keju* expanded political access to a broader segment of the population and promoted upward mobility.

Borrowing terminologies from the "selectorate" theory in De Mesquita et al. (2005), *Keju* essentially expanded the selectorate. By increasing the pool of eligible candidates for office, *Keju* rendered each member of the monarch's "inner circle" more replaceable and, consequently, more reliant on the monarch (Huang and Yang, 2022). We demonstrate with extensive evidence in the following sections that this political function withstood the test of time with a surprising level of resilience. The magnitude of aristocratic advantage continued to decline, and the level of social mobility within the broader elite continued to rise over time. Moreover, leveraging a cross-country panel dataset, we show that the *Keju* was associated with an increase in ruler stability that was comparable to the impact of parliaments in Europe.

Keju was "proto-meritocratic." It had the aforementioned meritocratic tendencies, but the meritocracy was only "proto" because it primarily equalized opportunities within the broader elite, as many commoners were not wealthy enough to afford the books and time (away from agriculture) to prepare for the exams.[1] The term "proto" suggests a continuum, indicating that the system's capacity to equalize opportunities could either increase or decrease. Sections 3 and 4 detail efforts made by rulers to maintain *Keju*'s equalizing potential. These efforts included ad hoc but consistently applied affirmative actions against the powerful families during the 9th century, the narrowing of the curriculum and the standardization of exam format, and the expansion of the school system over the second millennium.

Keju was also *proto*-meritocratic because the exams might not test people's "true" competence. There was a considerable gap between what was being tested and the skills necessary for effective administration or statecraft. Candidates usually succeeded by writing highly formulaic and predictable answers within a predominantly Confucian framework. We clarify, however, in Section 5.2.4 that selection based on true competence is not a precondition for Argument 1 to hold. There could even be a potential trade-off between the equalizing dimension and the competence dimension of meritocracy: a hypothetically perfect device to identify "true" talents could quite possibly end up selecting the political know-hows, who would have predominantly come from families with officeholding traditions. History seems to suggest that, at times, the emperors were willing to sacrifice talent in favor of the equalizing effect.

Argument 2

However, it's crucial not to conflate the "effect" of an institution with its "origins" (Pierson, 2004). The long-term political consequences of *Keju* could hardly have been foreseen by powerholders in the late 6th and early 7th centuries when the system first took shape. Even though one of *Keju*'s key political consequences was to enhance the ruler's power vis-à-vis the upper elites, it is unlikely that the "designer" of *Keju*, if there was one to speak of, had this purpose in mind. And even if he did, *Keju* would not be able to achieve this goal

---

[1] Furthermore, the exams were only open to *males*.

until a century later. The *Keju* system, originating from gradual institutional change over the long durée since the 2nd-century CE, evolved in a context where events that now appear as "breakthroughs" were merely incremental steps at their time. The eventual development in 622 CE, which endowed the system with the potential to expand political access, emerged as a contingent response to urgent issues at the time, revealing a functional logic rather than a deliberate political strategy. Given the gradual nature of *Keju*'s development, its initial impact was minimal and difficult to discern, thus encountering little resistance. Over time, as its significance grew and in conjunction with unforeseen political developments, both the ruler and the elites came to view the institution as beneficial to their interests, thereby making *Keju* a self-enforcing institution. The emergence of *Keju* was a process, not a shock.

By treating *Keju* as both an outcome and a contributor to political development, and focusing on the positive feedback for the participants in the institution, our work borrows insights from the literature on historical institutionalism (Mahoney and Thelen, 2009). This Element presents the evolution of bureaucratic selection in imperial China as an excellent example of gradual institutional change over the very long run, in which *Keju* itself had attained at least 1,200 years of prominence. This process saw changes take place incrementally as rulers and elites responded to unforeseen and exogenous events.

1.2 *Keju* versus Parliament

A new scholarship in historical political economy now distinguishes between an institution's consequences from its origins, though much of this literature chiefly concerns with representative institutions. Recent studies demonstrate that the ruler-constraining and mass empowerment functions of modern parliaments differed from the purpose of their emergence, which was to collect information and assist governance for the ruler (Stasavage, 2020; Boucoyannis, 2021). Boucoyannis (2021), in particular, shows how national parliaments were initially judicial institutions employed by rulers to extend control over the population and territory. Its original purpose was not to constrain the crown, a completely opposite political function that only materialized much later. Similarly (and conversely), it was also unlikely that *Keju* was "invented" to undermine the aristocracy (Sections 2 and 3), a consequence that took almost a century to materialize.

Another similarity is that sufficient ruler strength is required for the consolidation of both institutions. In the European case, nobles initially resented the heavy burden of serving their judicial duties in the parliament for the ruler. The national parliament was successful in England because ruler strength there was the highest across European polities and enough to achieve "elite compellence"

(Boucoyannis, 2021). The Chinese emperor was *even more powerful* than the English monarch in the following sense. The upper elites in imperial Chinese history, for the most part, had to operate within a bureaucratic framework and derive their power, prestige, and, to some extent, wealth from bureaucratic performance, the ultimate evaluator of which was the ruler herself. It was in this context, as Section 3 documents, that the elites' pursuit of their own political benefit furthered their alignment with the *Keju*. Despite the similarly contingent origins, European parliaments would eventually become ruler-constraining and facilitate credible commitment to underpin high state capacity (Dincecco, 2017). In contrast, *Keju*'s long-term consequence was to further empower an already powerful monarchy, the absolutism of which eventually inhibited state development (Wang, 2022).

1.3 Organization of the Element

We substantiate our arguments by analyzing a diverse array of quantitative data and qualitative evidence, drawing on both primary materials and secondary literature. As this research studies a historical institution, we organize the sections in a semi-chronological order. We start with *Argument 2* in Sections 2 and 3 and end with *Argument 1* in Section 5, while the second half of Section 3 and most of Section 4 substantiate both arguments.

To give readers unfamiliar with Chinese history a concise context before exploring the detailed analysis of long-term institutional evolution, we include the following brief historical overview of the *Keju* system.

1.4 Brief Historical Overview

Before the consolidation of *Keju*, China's bureaucratic selection limited candidacy either formally or informally to a select few. The "Chaju" system, initiated in the 2nd-century BCE, involved local officials nominating individuals for entry into the bureaucracy via examination. The Nine-Rank Rectifying System (NRRS), dominant from the 3rd to 5th centuries, categorized men into different grades based on their virtue and pedigree, with entry into the bureaucracy largely reserved for those with high grades.

Keju began to take shape during the Sui dynasty (581–618 CE) as an outgrowth of previous recruitment methods, still restricting participation to those nominated by government officials. However, in 622 CE during the Tang dynasty (618–907 CE), the exam was opened to most men and continued to mature throughout the 7th–9th centuries.

The Song dynasty (960–1279 CE) refined the system by institutionalizing multiple levels of exams and strictly enforcing regional quotas. Participation further broadened at the societal level with the state's commitment to promoting broader education and advancements in printing technology. The Ming and Qing Dynasties (1368–1911 CE) further refined the *Keju* with more rigorous qualification exams and the widespread establishment of public schools to standardize preparation.

The system was abolished in 1905 as the Qing dynasty faced internal and external pressures, including modernization demands and Western colonialism.

2 The Origins

2.1 Motivation

The core of this Element begins in the year 622 CE, when a significant institutional change seemed to have happened to the *Keju*. By then, what would later be recognized as the *Keju* system had been in its nascent stage for approximately two to three decades, albeit participation in the examination was limited to individuals nominated by senior government officials. Now, with an imperial edict by Emperor Gaozu of the Tang dynasty (唐高祖), the examination had been made open to the majority of adult males. From the perspectives of social science grand narratives, this was a monumental development. It essentially represented a "selectorate expansion" (Huang and Yang, 2022). By enlarging the pool of potential bureaucratic candidates, the ruler increased his leverage over the existing elite, making them more reliant upon him (De Mesquita et al., 2005). Relatedly, it's also tempting to view this policy as a deliberate move to promote social mobility, a key contributor to political stability as theoretical work of authoritarian politics would have us believe (Leventoğlu, 2005; Jia, Roland, and Xie, 2023).

Intriguingly, what should have marked a paradigm shift in the politics of the then world's largest empire largely escaped mention in its standard histories. The paramount texts for the political history of the Tang dynasty, where this pivotal change occurred, are the *Old Book of Tang* (《旧唐书》), *New Book of Tang* (《新唐书》), and *Comprehensive Mirror in Aid of Governance* (《资治通鉴》). These texts meticulously document many significant policy shifts of the dynasty, but this particular transition is conspicuously absent.[2]

More intriguingly, not a single historical source from the Tang makes mention of *resistance* or even debate regarding this policy. This notable silence stands in stark contrast to the grand narratives presented in social sciences about

---

[2] The exact imperial edict can be located in a corner of a vast encyclopedia of documents titled *Models from the Archives* (《册府元龟》), a resource less commonly utilized by political historians compared to the previously mentioned three canons.

the *Keju*. For instance, a recent publication, specifically attributing the *Keju* as the primary cause of the "Great Divergence" between China and the West, describes this reform as possessing a transformative potential that "few actions in human history can match" (Huang, 2023, p.43).[3] The same book also posits that this shift in policy was a calculated move to "disrupt, weaken, and decimate the incumbent aristocratic class" (p. 41). If there were indeed a single class so powerful as to be "incumbent," why didn't its members resist, or at least voice some complaints, about this dramatic shock?

Of course, we should not automatically equate the lack of recorded activities, be it discussions, debates, or resistance, with the lack of activities. It's possible that any resistance or dissent from the aristocrats was omitted or erased from the records. Another possibility is that the records from the Tang are simply scarce, given that the event of interest transpired over 1,400 years ago. Naturally, the farther back we look, the fewer records remain. However, both scenarios are unlikely. The chief compilers of neither *Old Book of Tang* nor *New Book of Tang* were "aristocrats" by Tang standards. If anything, they were emblematic of the new elite that emerged from the 10th century onwards through *Keju*, long after the influence of the Tang dynasty aristocracy had already waned (Lu, 2016; Wen, Wang, and Hout, 2024). The author of *Comprehensive Mirror* was in the same category. For the argument's sake, suppose that the purpose of manipulating history here was to protect the reputation of the "villains" in this event, the Tang aristocrats. Then post-Tang new elites would be the last one to do so. Had there been any dissenting views voiced by the aristocrats in 622 CE, the chroniclers of Tang history would be the least likely to hide them in protection of the aristocrats' reputation. Indeed, 11th-century writers, like the authors of *Comprehensive Mirror* and *New Book of Tang*, were actually quite keen on casting aristocrats in a negative light.[4] Equally importantly, critiques of *Keju* are actually quite prevalent across historical records covering the Tang, so it is also unlikely that the absence of recorded debate suggests that the

---

[3] Note that Huang (2023) is unclear about the exact year in which this reform took place. It seems likely that the book mis-attributed this reform to Emperor Wen of Sui in 587 CE. The book's description of *Keju*, especially its *explicit* emphasis on candidates' self-nomination (with the exact Chinese characters also listed) (*submitting materials and self-recommendations* (投碟自举), p. 43), indicates that the particular policy is the one in 622 CE. For the most recent historical discussion on this policy, see Lou (2019).

[4] Modern historians have long contended that the *Comprehensive Mirror* selectively combined primary records to present a biased view of Li Deyu (787–850 CE), member of a prominent aristocratic family and son of a Tang chief minister. The bias was especially salient when important policy disputes between Li and another high-ranking official, one of a much humbler background, were described (Fu, 2023). The section on *Keju*'s institutional history in the *New Book of Tang* also critiqued Li for allegedly advocating for descendants of powerful officials to be placed in powerful positions in the bureaucracy.

later compilers, despite their ascension through this system, intended to deflect criticisms about *Keju*.

More generally speaking, the Chinese historiography is not at all shy of recording the details of policy change, or the vigorous controversies, debates, and objections that might follow suit. A casual reader of imperial Chinese history could immediately think of the Wang Anshi Reform (王安石变法) in the mid-11th century, the "Single Whip" Reform (一条鞭法), and the submersion of the poll tax within the land tax (摊丁入亩) in early 18th century, all of which met fierce resistance from the vested interests.[5] Even prior to the Tang dynasty, when historical records were scarcer, there are detailed discussions of reforms that challenged the established powerholders, such as the Monopoly over Salt and Iron in the late 2nd-century BCE (Wagner, 2001) and the state-building reform in the late 5th century that laid the foundation for the country's reunification later on (Chen, Wang, and Zhang, 2025).

The Tang dynasty where the selectorate expansion via *Keju* happened was an era of great transformation. Numerous policies instituting profound changes were enacted in the dynasty. Some of them, such as the "Two-Tax Reform" (两税法) of 780 CE and the reform of 819 CE that divided military authority in the provinces, have recently been subjects of quantitative political science research (Wang, 2022; Chen and Wang, 2024). The former, in particular, was highly controversial and intense debates and critiques have been well-documented in the records.[6] The latter, while itself not causing much controversy, was set in motion in a larger context where the Tang rulers became increasingly intolerant of rebellious military commissioners in the provinces (Chen and Wang, 2024). Debates and conflicts between the "doves" and "hawks" toward the provinces were on full display from the historical records.[7]

Given the depth of Chinese historiography on policy reforms, the silence on the 622 CE *Keju* change is revealing. Perhaps the most logical interpretation is that the resistance from the powerholders, in this case the aristocrats, was indeed negligible. The lack of opposition or even discussion is puzzling in hindsight. Both the evidence in Sections 3 and 4 and the works by others reviewed in this Element, including Huang (2023), suggest that *Keju* would go on to have a profound impact. However, from the eyes of the early 7th-century beholders, such as the Tang aristocrats and even the emperor himself, it might not appear

---

[5] See Wang (2022) for quantitative analyses of resistance to the first two reforms.
[6] For example, Lu Zhi (陆贽), a prominent chief minister at the time, had made various arguments against the Two-Tax Reform at court. Wang (2022) provides a sociopolitical interpretation of the documented controversies over the policy.
[7] Such cleavages were occasionally intertwined with controversies over *Keju* in the 9th century. See Wang (2018) for a full discussion.

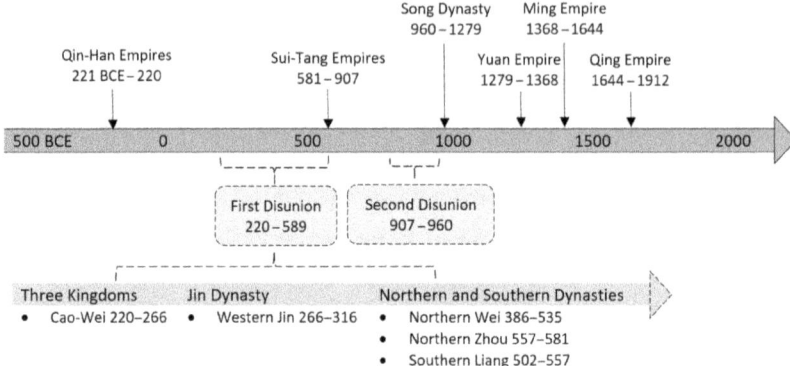

Figure 1 Timeline of regimes studied in the Element

as if anything transformative had happened. The imperial edict in 622 CE, as we argue, was simply an incremental step in the *longue durée* of gradual institutional change over the course of medieval Chinese history. Rather than a jolting change, it might well have been perceived as a continuation of past developments, thus not triggering vigorous discussion, let alone fierce opposition.

The rest of this section and Section 3 explain the origins and early development of *Keju*. This section documents the gradual institutional evolution of China's bureaucratic selection system prior to the 7th century. Section 3 addresses the evolution of *Keju* in the second half of the 7th century, focusing on the rising importance of this institution under Empress Wu. It then employs both quantitative and qualitative evidence to show how *Keju* eventually became a self-reinforcing institution in which both the ruler and the elites saw benefits from participating. These sections integrate insights from historical institutionalism (e.g. Mahoney, Thelen et al., 2009) to focus on institutional layering and positive feedback that made *Keju* eventually self-reinforcing. A key takeaway from this section is that institutional changes that are ex post transformative like the *Keju* should often be understood as a *process*, not a shock. This understanding is also in line with recent findings on the emergence of European parliaments (Boucoyannis, 2021).

As this Element, especially in this section, extensively mentions numerous polities in Chinese history, Figure 1 presents a timeline featuring the relevant regimes.

2.2 Gradual Institutional Change Over the *Long Durée* (The 2nd-Century BCE to 622 CE)

We begin by examining the historical evolution of methods and institutions for bureaucratic selection prior to the *Keju*. The narrative focuses on two primary methods: one based on exams, though participation was limited to a select few; and the other based on pedigree, with those assessing pedigree also belonging to a privileged group. Chronologically, the latter method was layered on top of the former, although the exam-based approach was never completely crowded out. In the 6th century, however, there was a reversal of fortune between the two methods. The exam-based approach began to rise again, with the emergence of *Keju* viewed as an outgrowth of this revival.

Throughout this *long durée* of institutional change, it is undeniable that rulers were concerned about political selection coming under the control of a small group of privileged elites. However, our account emphasizes other, more functionalist factors, such as the need to reassert central government authority over localities and to recruit talent in the absence of reliable information. These factors were arguably more pivotal to the eventual emergence of *Keju*, which, in any case, was unlikely viewed by contemporaries as a transformative strategy by the ruler to undermine the aristocracy.

2.2.1 Han Dynasty (202 BCE to 220 CE): Exam for the Nominated

Although exams were a defining feature of *Keju*, recruiting bureaucrats through examinations was not new in imperial China. In fact, the practice dates back to the Former Han dynasty (202 to 9 CE), the "time zero" of our historical explanation for the rise of *Keju* (Bielenstein, 1986). It was the first durable empire in Chinese history and employed a sizable bureaucracy (Zhao, 2015). The recruitment system for this bureaucracy was *Chaju* (察举制), which further matured in the Later Han dynasty (25–220 CE). Under this approach, imperial officials would identify individuals in possession of high morals or talent within their local jurisdictions and then nominate these individuals to sit for an examination in the capital. Upon successful completion of this test, the nominees would be recruited into the bureaucracy (Doran, 2017).

In some aspects, exams were even more crucial for bureaucratic selection under the *Chaju* system during the Han than under the *Keju* system in the Tang. During the 7th–9th centuries, success in *Keju* exams only made an examinee a candidate for imperial bureaucracy, with actual appointments depending on a separate vetting process by the Ministry of Personnel (吏部), often leading to significant delays and challenges (Lai, 2008).[8] In contrast, passing a *Chaju* exam more directly and swiftly led to official positions.

As emphasized earlier, the transformative aspect of *Keju* lies not in the use of exams *per se* but in the broader eligibility for exam participation. Under *Chaju*,

---

[8] Tang epitaphs even reveal that 7% of *Keju* degree holders *never* achieved a ranked office throughout the entire lifetime (Wen, Wang, and Hout, 2024).

exam takers were limited to a select few, as only those nominated by officials were allowed to participate. The predominant method of political selection from the 2nd-century BCE to the 2nd-century CE could be described as "exam for the nominated."

In Later Han, *Chaju* increasingly relied on the collective opinion of elite society in each locality to recruit new blood into the bureaucracy. Local notables in each prefecture held gatherings akin to social clubs, where they discussed and provided informal *ratings* for young men in their locality (Zhang, 2015). These ratings, though never standardized across elite societies in different prefectures, were broadly based on the men's possession of morals and talents as perceived by the local elite.[9] As prefects in the Han took very seriously the opinion of the local elites (Brown and Xie, 2015), the rise of an informal local "rating" system heavily influenced bureaucratic selection via the *Chaju*.

As the Han empire crumbled in the late 2nd century amidst civil wars, its successors faced a deeply flawed *Chaju* system. Functionally, the system struggled as wars and upheaval dispersed local elites, disrupting the collective assessments crucial for individual ratings. Politically, the new rulers viewed the system's reliance on local elite opinion for appointments as a threat, fearing it could lead to state capture by localist interests.

2.2.2 The 3rd to 5th Centuries CE: Nine-Rank Rectifying System

This subsection explains the rise of another recruitment institution that was originally designed to resolve the flaws of the examination-based *Chaju* system. Its core mechanics, however, soon rendered the new institution equally (if not more) prone to state capture by the politically and socially privileged few.

By the early 3rd century, the fragmented warlord territories in northern China were progressively unified under the leadership of Cao Cao (曹操). Cao sought to remedy the functional and political shortcomings of the Later Han *Chaju*, while still incorporating the more recent development of individual rating practices. The resultant "Nine-Rank Rectifying System" (九品中正制, hereafter NRRS) was initially an effort to address both challenges. Acknowledging the absence of a stable elite society due to the civil wars and mass migrations, Cao strategically appointed members from the *most prominent clans* of each region to identify and recruit local talents for his government. This approach was based on the belief that these prominent clans were more resilient and retained their influence despite the turmoil of war and disasters, and, as a result, they would

---

[9] Chinese dynastic histories feature many biographies of elites known as effective "raters" of men. Typically, these elites would be described as "skilled in ranking men according to their qualities" (善人伦) or "fond of ranking men according to their qualities" (好人伦).

remain as the best "know-how" and "know-who"s in the region and could offer valuable information for bureaucratic selection (Zhang, 2015). Politically, the prestigious elites appointed for such roles were, by definition, Cao's own government officials. This way, Cao made sure that those in charge of assessing and recruiting local talents shared with him the same political vision.[10]

A historian writing in the late 5th-century CE considered Cao's invention to be just an "ad hoc" (权立) solution.[11] Yet, toward the end of Cao's reign, this assessment method had become formalized into a system where male individuals from each locality would expect an assessment of his quality from the government (Zhang, 2015). It was his son Cao Pi (曹丕), the founder of the "Cao-Wei" dynasty, who fully institutionalized this new method of bureaucratic selection around 220 CE (Ebrey, 1978).

A simplified description of the NRRS is as follows. Each locality had a "rectifier" (中正) responsible for evaluating the "quality" of local men. Every three years, rectifiers would assign a grade from one to nine (hence the phrase "nine-rank" in the name of the system) to each educated male, with higher grades indicating superior quality. These assessments were then forwarded to a higher-level government organ for approval (e.g. Ebrey, 1978; Zhang, 2015).

When applying for government positions, individuals were assigned entry-level roles by the Ministry of Personnel based on their most recent quality grades. These entry-level positions varied significantly in office rank, importance, and prestige. Generally, individuals with higher quality grades received more prestigious entry-level positions with higher office ranks. Starting from these positions often led to advancement to senior roles in the national bureaucracy, reaching the pinnacle of political power. Notably, these quality grades influenced not only initial bureaucratic placements but also the peak positions attainable in one's career. Individuals with higher quality grades faced no "cap" on their career advancement, whereas those with lower grades were typically confined to lower bureaucratic levels for life.

Initially, the NRRS seemed to be a highly centralized system (Tang, 2010; Zhang, 2015). A rectifier's appointment must satisfy two eligibility conditions. One is that the appointee must originate from the locality in question. The other is that the person holding the rectifier position must be a *central* government official holding the post concurrently. The second requirement thus

---

[10] Many of such officials were highly capable administrators and strategists who would play a key role in helping the House of Cao consolidate its rule and rebuild the state in northern China.
[11] *Book of Song*, vol. 94.

built upon Cao Cao's practice of having government officials, rather than local elites outside the political system, make evaluations of men's quality.[12]

However, the NRRS soon fell under the control of local "aristocrats," a term commonly referring to prestigious and wealthy landed families (such as the prominent clans mentioned earlier) from the 3rd to 6th centuries (Ebrey, 1978). Typically, those selected as local rectifiers belonged to these families, as they held the cultural and moral high ground and possessed unparalleled knowledge about their locality. As one could expect, these aristocrats often assigned high grades to their own kind in the locality, who then entered civil service through prestigious and advantageous posts, conducive to further career advancement. Once these individuals secured influential positions in the bureaucracy, capable of impacting the appointment of rectifiers, they tended to favor their own kind for such roles. This practice perpetuated a cycle of intergenerational aristocratic advantage in officeholding (e.g. Miyazaki, 1977; Tang, 2010; Zhang, 2015).

2.2.3 The 6th-Century CE: Decline of the NRRS and the Revival of the Examination Method

This subsection documents the decline of the NRRS and the corresponding revival of exams as a recruitment method. It emphasizes that the *Chaju* system was never abandoned but simply became less prominent. The rise of NRRS as part of China's recruitment system should thus be seen as institutional layering (Mahoney, Thelen et al., 2009). When different polities in the 6th century gradually downplayed or even repurposed the NRRS, we see that the examination method became prominent again, and the eventual emergence of *Keju* is arguably an outgrowth of this trend of revival.

There are two prevalent misconceptions in recent social science works on early *Keju*. The first is that examinations were "discontinued" from the 3rd to 6th centuries as the NRRS "arose to replace" the *Chaju* (Huang, 2023, pp. 32–33). The second misconception, reflected in the likes of Chen, Fan, and Huang (2023), is that the NRRS remained the dominant method of bureaucratic recruitment until the exogenous introduction of *Keju*. However, these assertions are in fact fundamental misunderstandings.

Examinations were *never* discontinued as a recruitment method between the 3rd and 6th centuries. What happened was akin to institutional layering (Mahoney, Thelen et al., 2009). Just as in the Han dynasty, those individuals nominated by local officials, once passing the exam, could still begin their

---

[12] That quality ranks had to be reviewed and approved by a high organ in the central government, the Office of the Excellency over the Masses (司徒府), is another layer of centralized control.

careers in the bureaucracy swiftly.[13] *Chaju* did take a back seat from the 3rd to 5th centuries, when the majority of elites who would eventually secure ranked positions in the bureaucracy entered the civil service through the NRRS route. In contrast, those who entered via the *Chaju* typically secured less prestigious entry-level positions and consequently had limited career progression. Individuals opting for the *Chaju* route often came from relatively modest backgrounds (Zhang, 2015). However, starting from the late 5th century, the situation began to shift significantly in both north and south.

Northern Wei (386–535 CE): The NRRS Declined While *Chaju* Became Prominent Again

The Cao–Wei regime in the north was later toppled by the House of Sima, leading to the brief Western Jin dynasty (266–316 CE), which conquered the south but soon fell apart due to internal strife and pressures from the so-called barbarian groups who originated beyond the imperial frontiers. In the ensuing chaos, a Sima prince founded the Eastern Jin dynasty (317–420 CE) in today's Nanjing, controlling the empire's southern half. This period transitioned into the Southern Dynasties era (420–589 CE), marked by successive regimes in the south.

Meanwhile, numerous warring kingdoms in northern China, founded in the aftermath of Western Jin's collapse, struggled to exert control over rural areas, which had become turfs of the powerful local aristocrats. In the late 4th century, nomadic warriors from the steppes established the Northern Wei dynasty (386–535 CE) under the House of Tuoba, soon conquering other northern kingdoms. A major reform in 485–486 CE allowed Northern Wei to impose direct rule over the countryside. To compensate for the aristocrats' loss of local autonomy, the regime integrated them into the national bureaucracy, converting them from local powerholders into stakeholders of the imperial state (Chen, Wang, and Zhang, 2025).

Revival of *Chaju* was key to the recruitment of local aristocrats. From the late 5th century onward, the number of elites who entered civil service through *Chaju* dramatically increased. Unlike prior regimes and southern dynasties, where *Chaju* was left to those of lower birth, in the Northern Wei dynasty, aristocrats eagerly participated in *Chaju* (Yan, 2021). Perhaps the most remarkable change was the rapid rise of *Chaju* as a predictor of career success. According to Yan (2021), among the fifty-five elites who entered the civil service through the *xiucai* examination (a category of *Chaju* for which we have the

---

[13] Examination during this era now also served an additional function: Individuals could *improve* their qualified grades that were originally given by their local rectifiers via participating in the *Chaju* exams (Wang, 1995; Zhang, 2015).

most comprehensive data), a significant 82.1% achieved ranks above Rank Five Junior.[14] Furthermore, an impressive 52.3% reached positions above Rank Three Junior, a threshold distinguishing senior government roles.[15]

Yan (2021) also collects data for imperial and national academy *students* in Northern Wei. The academy system had been part of the broader *Chaju* institution since the Han dynasty, where students who studied in imperially sanctioned venues in the national capital could enter civil service upon passing an exam. When the Northern Wei regime revived the *Chaju*, it boosted the academy system as well. Among the forty-seven students for whom the data were available, a stunning 96% attained positions above Rank Five Junior, and 61.9% surpassed the Rank Three Junior threshold. Northern Wei, the regime that laid the foundation for the unified Sui and Tang empires where *Keju* took shape (e.g. Huang, 1996; Yan, 2017), witnessed the resurgence of the examination method as a prevalent and the most elitist route to the bureaucracy.

Meanwhile, the Northern Wei regime undermined the primacy of the NRRS in various ways. The first is its underutilization. Recall that, via the Reform of 485–486 CE, the regime imposed direct rule over areas that local aristocrats once enjoyed autonomy. As a part of the political deal, the Northern Wei rulers disproportionately recruited aristocrats from these areas into the upper echelon of the imperial bureaucracy. This was a crucial episode of Chinese history in which rulers substantially increased state penetration at the local level via a "compensation" package that transformed the erstwhile local powerholders into national stakeholders (Chen, Wang, and Zhang, 2025). These compensated aristocrats became more likely, during and after the Reform, to take a variety of important, prestigious, and powerful offices at both national and regional levels, even including ones that could constrain the rulers' own power (Chen, Wang, and Zhang, 2025). One may naturally expect that the rectifier positions central to the NRRS would also be used by rulers in this master stroke of political maneuvering, but it was not the case at all.[16]

Besides its diminishing role as a political tool, the prestige of the NRRS also appeared to erode during the Northern Wei period. Notably, the Tuoba emperors began appointing two groups of men from humble backgrounds to rectifier positions. The first group comprised individuals who, in the eyes of the elite

---

[14] Rank Five Junior marks the division between upper-level and lower-level officials in the Chinese bureaucracy.

[15] These percentages for the *xiucai* examination group are both higher than those for the broader universe of known elites, where the rates are 73.1% and 48.5% for attaining positions above Rank Five Junior and Rank Three Junior, respectively (Chen, Wang, and Zhang, 2025).

[16] Specifically, the estimated increase in the likelihood of these aristocrats taking the rectifier positions after the Reform of 485–486 CE is both substantively and significantly insignificant (Chen, Wang, and Zhang, 2025).

society, had apparently fabricated their aristocratic identities.[17] The second group consisted of *eunuchs* (Yan, 2021). This shift was particularly striking, considering that, traditionally, rectifier positions were exclusive to elites with distinguished family pedigrees. Yet now, it appears that even those considered the most despised in Chinese history could become rectifiers!

Northern Zhou (557–581 CE): The NRRS Became Largely Ceremonial

It was under Northern Zhou that the NRRS became completely sidelined. Zhou was a new regime in northwestern China that arose from the division of Northern Wei in 534 CE under the House of Yuwen. By 579 CE, the Yuwens had unified much of northern China and laid critical political groundwork for the subsequent centuries under the Sui and Tang Dynasties, with the Sui established in 581 CE via a palace coup.

Critically, the emerging consensus in historical research suggests that Northern Zhou rulers completely repurposed the NRRS to a ceremonial system, with rectifiers serving in decorative roles rather than their former bureaucratic recruitment function. The examination method via *Chaju* continued to rise until it blossomed into *Keju* in the early 7th century.[18] Contrary to the aforementioned misunderstandings, *Keju* did not "replace" the NRRS. There was a significant hiatus between the founding of Northern Zhou and 605–607 CE (discussed next) when *Keju* was allegedly introduced, during which the NRRS was already marginalized and *Chaju* was in full use. The emergence of *Keju* therefore followed a much more gradual process than a "replacement."

Parallel to the institutional evolution in the north was a similar process in the south, where the rulers fostered "selectorate expansion" by making a qualification exam for entering the bureaucracy open to most adult males in 509 CE. This development was also built on the gradual revival of examination via *Chaju* even though the NRRS in the south remained vital unlike in Northern Zhou (Yan, 2021). It should now become even clearer that selectorate expansion through examination could and did evolve from *Chaju*'s revival and that it did not occur as a replacement of the NRRS.

2.2.4 *Keju in 605–607 and 622 CE*

This subsection explores the early development of the *Keju* system, highlighting how it was more a continuation of gradual institutional changes rather than a revolutionary shift. *Keju* in the early Tang era carried the legacy of nomination

---
[17] Notable examples are discussed in *Book of Wei*, vol. 93.
[18] For the further marginalization of the NRRS under Northern Zhou, see Huang (2014, 2016a). For how Northern Zhou repurposed the rectifiers, see Guo (2019).

and recommendation from the *Chaju* system, and was in fact an outgrowth of *Chaju*. It thus remained limited as a recruitment tool. This gradual evolution suggests that the modest changes in 622 CE were unlikely to have been seen as transformative in the eyes of the beholders.

The institution later known as the *Keju* formally began in the early 7th century. However, pinpointing the exact year of its inception has been a subject of intense debate among historians. This debate primarily revolves around multiple proposed dates. Dominant among these are the perspectives of the "pro-Sui camp" and the "pro-Tang camp." The pro-Tang camp's rationale is straightforward: They argue that the *Keju*, known for offering individuals from modest backgrounds a chance to compete, could only have started when examinees were allowed to participate through *self*-nomination. In their view, *Keju* began when it was no longer the *Chaju*, examination for those nominated by government officials. For them, *Keju* began when it "expanded" in 622 CE, under the Tang dynasty, for the exact reason discussed in the beginning of this section.[19] On the other hand, the pro-Sui camp suggests two possibilities: 587 and 605–607 CE, with the latter receiving more emphasis.[20] In 605–607 CE, the examination category known as *Jinshi* (进士科) was introduced.[21] By the late imperial China (14th to 19th centuries), *Jinshi* had become synonymous with the highest and final degree of the *Keju* examination.

The very existence of this debate itself is important for social scientists interested in institutions. It suggests that significant institutions like the *Keju* often do not emerge as sudden, transformative shocks with immediate impact. If the *Keju* had been such a pivotal institution effecting immediate change upon its inception, then its founding year, and specifically what kind of institutional changes should really constitute as the inception of *Keju*, would likely not be as disputed. By examining these years chronologically, we demonstrate that neither marked a significant change at their respective times. Rather, the developments in these early years of the 7th century were simply a continuation of the long history of gradual institutional change that began in the Han dynasty and continued until the end of the 6th century, as documented earlier.

Between 605 and 607 CE, Emperor Yang of the Sui dynasty (隋炀帝) promulgated a series of edicts that some modern historians cite as marking the inception of *Keju*.[22] A detailed examination of these edicts reveals that this

---

[19] See a discussion of this rationale in He (2000).
[20] For a discussion, see the third section of chapter 1 in Jin (2015).
[21] We use the bundle "605–607 CE" because in both 605 and 607 CE there were edicts issued by the same emperor that historians later would use as evidence that the *Jinshi* exam was created. Note that historians continue to debate what exactly happened, institutionally, under this emperor (in 605–607 and more generally) with respect to the inception of *Keju*.
[22] Refer to the literature review in Liu (2000) for further discussion on this topic.

so-called inception was more a continuation of an existing trend rather than a new beginning.[23] In 605 CE, Emperor Yang decreed that officials should "identify and recruit talent based on their abilities" within their respective jurisdictions. This decree also included a provision for talented individuals who chose not to join the bureaucracy, stipulating that such individuals should still receive a state salary "proportional to their abilities and their family pedigree."[24] In 607 CE, the emperor issued another edict, part of which simply said: "Those who hold government positions at Rank Five or above should nominate people to participate in one of the ten categories of the imperial examination."[25] Taken together, these two edicts do not reveal any significant departure from the *Chaju* tradition since the Han dynasty. The eligibility for the imperial examination continued to be limited to individuals nominated by government officials. Thus, the Imperial Examination System of the Sui dynasty appears as a natural progression of the *Chaju* system. This evolution should be viewed in the context of the revival of *Chaju* and the decline of the NRRS over Northern Wei and Northern Zhou, the predecessors of Sui regime. In short, the institutions "created" in 605–607 CE were, just as *Chaju* was, *exam for the nominated*. The 607 edict is of particular importance because there seems to be a technical connection between this edict and the one in 622 CE marking the selectorate expansion, which we address next.

In 622 CE, as previously mentioned, Emperor Gaozu of Tang issued an edict expanding the *Keju* system. The provisions regarding imperial examinations in this edict closely resembled those from the 607 CE edict, with both requiring officials of "Rank Five" and above to nominate talented individuals.[26] The edict of 622 CE, however, included a minor addition at the end: "those talents not nominated by these officials should self-nominate to participate (in the exams)."[27]

---

[23] Most historians who participate in this "dating" debate agree that, regardless of *when Keju* began, it began as a continuation of prior institutional development. We will discuss this point later.

[24] *Book of Sui*, vol. 3. The original Chinese text states: 诸在家及见入学者，若有笃志好古，耽悦典坟，学行优敏，堪膺时务，所在采访，具以名闻，即当随其器能，擢以不次。若研精经术，未愿进仕者，可依其艺业深浅，门荫高卑，虽未升朝，并量准给禄。

[25] *Book of Sui*, vol. 3. The original text in Chinese is: 文武有职事者，五品已上，宜依令十科举人。

[26] A slight variation exists in the wording concerning the rank cutoff in the 607 edict. Instead of generically stating "those holding government positions at Rank Five or above," as its predecessor did, it specifies "those in *central* government positions at Rank Five or above, as well as regional commissioners and prefects." However, all regional commissioners and prefects in the Tang dynasty were ranked above Rank Five. This minor change in wording does not significantly alter the meaning.

[27] The original Chinese text is: "宜令京官五品以上及诸州总管刺史各举一人其有志行可录才用未申亦听自举。"

There are several reasons to doubt that the developments in 622 CE would have been perceived as revolutionary at the time. First, these developments were a direct continuation of the preceding institutional changes, particularly the revival of recruitment through examinations and the decline of NRRS. Second, the 622 edict essentially built upon its 607 predecessor, with the addition of self-nomination – a discernible yet minor refinement – appearing only at the end of the provision regarding the imperial examination.

One way to appreciate the minimal nature of this step is by examining the composition of top officials in the Tang dynasty. During the reigns of the first two emperors, when this selectorate expansion occurred, fewer than 22% of chief ministers entered the bureaucracy initially through *Keju*. Among these six chief ministers, five had prestigious family background, with only one being a complete outsider to the system.[28] Data from Tang dynasty epitaphs, representing a broader elite spectrum, paints a similar picture (Wen, Wang, and Hout, 2024). Among the elites who passed away before 649 (the end of the second Tang emperor's reign), only 3.8% held a *Keju* credential. Throughout the 7th century, merely 8% of new recruits into the bureaucracy had *Keju* credentials. In short, statistics from both the highest echelons of political power and the broader elite society reveal that *Keju*'s role in early Tang politics was not only quite limited as a tool for general recruitment, but it also predominantly functioned as a pathway for the powerful few to attain office, even following the expansion in 622.

These figures should not be surprising to those familiar with early Tang history, where the nascent examination system continued the legacy of nomination, and the political selection process still mirrored the entrenched interests of the incumbent elite. A notable instance is the case of Zhang Chujin (张楚金), who was selected by his local government to take the imperial exam in the capital, over his brother. Zhang offered to relinquish this opportunity, arguing to the local authorities that his brother was more talented. This act caught the attention of Xu Shiji (徐世绩), a regional superintendent and high-ranking government official, who intervened to have both brothers nominated for the exam. Xu, a distinguished founding elite of the Tang dynasty and a close ally of the first two emperors, had earned the privilege of adopting the imperial surname "Li." The Zhang brothers were related to another high-ranking founding elite, once a colleague of Xu in the central government.

---

[28] These statistics were taken from the tabulations in Jin (2015), which uses a single-dimension definition of aristocrats that combines both patronage and prestige. More sophisticated quantitative analyses later in this section will take the two-dimensional approach in Wen, Wang, and Hout (2024).

While Tang historical records depict this episode as demonstrating Zhang's talent and humility, and Xu's knack for recognizing true talent, it also unwittingly reveals how patronage and privilege could manipulate the system. Notably, the record ends with the phrase "he nominated both to *pass the final exam*" (emphasis added).[29] This implies that, from the perspective of Tang contemporaries, Xu's intervention was seen as ensuring their success in the final stage of the exam, not just their chance to participate. More significantly, this episode highlights that despite the 622 *Keju* expansion allowing for self-nomination, the long-standing tradition of *Chaju*, particularly nominations by government officials, continued to play a pivotal role in the examination system.

To sum up, by documenting the abundant primary and secondary evidence, this subsection demonstrates that the beginning of *Keju* was very much a continuation of gradual institutional change over the *long durée*. The legacy of prior institutions, especially the *Chaju* system, still loomed large in the early years of *Keju*. Furthermore, in the early Tang era, *Keju*'s role was quite constrained both in and of itself as a recruitment institution and as a political tool to expand the selectorate. Its limited use appeared to be practically (though not legally) restricted to those with patronage and power. Consequently, it seems highly improbable that the modest adjustment in 622 CE (and even less so in 605 or 607 CE) was regarded as a groundbreaking change by the "aristocrats," however they are defined.[30] Instead, the bulk of evidence points toward a "business as usual" sentiment prevailing among the elite of that era.

2.2.5 Keju *as Ad Hoc Solution*

While it's challenging to ascertain the emperor's exact intentions behind the 622 *Keju* expansion, attributing it solely to an effort to undermine the aristocracy overlooks a more plausible functionalist explanation that is well aligned with critical political developments preceding the Tang. A notable trend was the

---

[29] *Old Book of Tang*, vol. 187. The original Chinese text is 乃俱荐擢第. The *Old Book* was compiled in the early 10th century, featuring a portrayal of the event similar to that in a mid-9th-century source, as cited in the *Extensive Records of the Taiping Era*, also from the 10th century. The earliest reference to this event is found in an early 9th century work, the *New Anecdotes of the Tang Dynasty*, which, interestingly, limits Xu's nomination to merely the eligibility for the capital exam, not its eventual success. Furthermore, an analysis of the variations in wording used to describe this event across the three sources, each from distinct eras, suggests that the *Keju* system in the early Tang period was quite under-institutionalized compared to its later variant in the mid and late Tang periods. However, a detailed exploration of this aspect falls outside the scope of this Element.

[30] The two social science works that assert grand causal claims about the early *Keju* undermining the "aristocrats" or "nobles" do not define "aristocrats" (Huang, 2023) or "nobles" (Chen, Fan, and Huang, 2023).

administrative and political *centralization* initiated during the Northern Zhou period and pursued vigorously by the Sui. This legacy of centralization was inherited by the Tang and would persist throughout the subsequent history of imperial China for over a millennium. It's beyond the scope of this work to elaborate on these policies in detail, but the essence of the most pivotal one was that, previously, prefects had the autonomy to appoint their own staff, typically drawn from local elites, for their prefecture governments. Now, the central government appointed virtually all officials within the prefecture government. This shift was viewed as a transformational strategy that significantly redirected power from local governments and local elites toward the central government (e.g. Ebrey, 1978; Jin, 2015). However, this change undoubtedly placed a burden on the central government to devise mechanisms for official selection, as officials even at the very local level now required direct appointment from the center.[31] *Keju*, though still in its early stages, emerged as one of the centralized responses to this need for centralized recruitment.[32]

Another significant trend is the migration of local aristocrats to the imperial capitals, a phenomenon referred to as the "centralization of the aristocracy." This movement began in the late 5th century (Chen, Wang, and Zhang, 2025), intensified during the 6th century (Ebrey, 1978), and by the 8th century, most Chinese aristocrats had severed ties with their original hometowns (Tackett, 2020). Such developments challenge the notion that the emergence of *Keju*, particularly as a substitute for the NRRS, aimed to undermine the "aristocracy." To the extent that the NRRS and *Chaju* benefited the aristocrats, it's because both systems were locally organized in a way that particularly put aristocrats into the formal (as in NRRS) or informal (as in *Chaju*) position to favorably grade (as in NRRS) or nominate (as in *Chaju*) their own kind from the same locality for political office. Their relevance for the reproduction of political power by the aristocrats (allegedly for generations) now diminished as aristocrats became less localized. Consequently, the discontinuation of the

---

[31] Historians studying the institutional origins of *Keju* overwhelmingly focus on functional explanations similar to the one advanced here. For example, Wu (1992) highlights the severe mismatch between the skill distribution of the extant officials and the talents deemed necessary for the management of the Sui empire in late 6th century, specifically regarding the construction of institutions, rituals, and laws. Sui emperors developed *Keju* to address such needs (pp. 4–9).

[32] We have previously highlighted the *Keju* in 605–607 CE and 622 CE as a continuation of the *Chaju* tradition. Nonetheless, the *Keju* edicts of 607 and 622 CE depart from the *Chaju* of the 2nd century in a critical way: While *Keju* at the time predominantly relied on nomination (just like *Chaju*), the pool of nominators included both capital and local officials, in contrast to *Chaju* in the 2nd century, which primarily delegated local officials to nominate talents from their local jurisdictions. Over time, *Chaju* evolved such that the nomination system became less tied to local jurisdictions (Yan, 2021).

NRRS (and similarly, *Chaju*) arguably did not significantly weaken aristocratic influence as much as some grand narratives suggest. In fact, the centralized nature of *Keju*, in this very sense, could be seen as beneficial to the aristocrats, now increasingly centralized in residence. Candidates from the capital enjoyed numerous advantages in the *Keju* (Fu, 2020).[33] The decline of the NRRS, once beneficial to local powerholders, occurred as aristocrats shifted from local powerholders to centralized elites. This transition, coupled with the rise of *Keju* that would favor centralized elites, suggests that *Keju*'s introduction was unlikely to undermine the aristocracy. This is not to say that *Keju* would not facilitate social mobility, which it did in the Tang (Section 3). Our argument is simply that the rationale for it was unlikely anti-aristocratic in as early as 605 or 622 CE.

The particular "breakthrough" in 622 likely reveals a functionalist logic as well. The Tang dynasty was founded in 618 as a series of peasant and elite rebellions destroyed the Sui empire. It was initially a regime based in Chang'an (长安) and its surrounding regions, but later reconquered the rest of China, then dominated by numerous rebellion leaders fighting with one another. There is abundant evidence that elites (outside the Guanlong "northwestern" regions) in the early years of the dynasty were uninterested in politics, perceived as unstable, chaotic, and dangerous.[34] The aforementioned centralization efforts of the Tang's predecessor regimes had already posed recruitment challenges for the Ministry of Personnel. Thus, the Tang faced particularly significant difficulties in political selection, especially given the urgent need to staff the new government amidst widespread chaos and uncertainty. Coupled with the unprecedented need for local talents was the lack of information allowing the rulers to identify them. The centralization of aristocrats and a century of elite migration amidst waves of wars and upheavals in the 6th century had only worsened the information gap. At one point, the founding emperor was so desperate that he even reinstated the NRRS in 624 CE so that "an aristocrat in each locality would be a rectifier to evaluate people's quality."[35] Yet, precisely because the aristocrats were no longer in their ancestral homes ("choronyms"), this initiative faltered and was quickly discontinued (Jin, 2015, p.38). It seemed only natural that amid the desperate need for talents and the severe lack of information to identify them, the edict in 622 would allow individuals to *self-nominate*. The method of examination, from an informational perspective, was now also more important than ever.

---

[33] Furthermore, regional quotas were poorly enforced, if not nonexistent, during the Tang (Jin, 2015), so the capital region never appeared too "crowded" for the aristocrats in terms of *Keju* competition.

[34] e.g. *Comprehensive Mirror*, vol. 192.

[35] *Comprehensive Mirror*, vol. 190.

To sum up, via detailed analysis of primary materials and secondary literature, we have highlighted the rise of *Keju* as a continuation of the gradual institutional change in early and medieval China over the *long durée*. The eventual breakthrough, the political effect of which could only manifest itself ex post (Sections 3 and 4), was most likely an ad hoc technical solution to new challenges in bureaucratic recruitment. The mechanism of institutional change in our account is similar to "layering" in historical institutionalism (e.g. Mahoney, Thelen et al., 2009). The initial policies that scholars would later attribute the *Keju* to could be best understood as new layers added to the *Chaju* system whose evolution had a reversal of fortune vis-à-vis the NRRS.

Our account also contributes to the theory of bureaucracy as a solution to address informational asymmetries between the ruler and the ruled (Stasavage, 2020). The bureaucratic solution would not be feasible if the initial level of information gap is prohibitively high: To recruit bureaucrats who would sustain the bureaucracy, one needs some information about local talents to begin with. In contexts where such knowledge was severely lacking, *Keju* arose as a solution.

Keju in 622 CE as *Magna Carta* in Reverse?

The *Keju* breakthrough in 622 CE, in our analysis, can be viewed as a *Magna Carta* moment in Chinese history, albeit in reverse. Like the royal Charter of 1215 CE, the edict issued by Emperor Gaozu had a profound impact on the balance of power between the ruler and the upper elites; however, in the Chinese case, the balance tilted in favor of the ruler rather than the nobles, as in the English context. The more significant similarity between these two moments is that the transformative nature of each could not have been envisaged by contemporaries. In England, it was subsequent political developments later in the century – such as "Henry III's minority, his foreign ambitions, his lack of funds, and the general unpopularity of his government" – that eventually elevated the Charter's importance in politics and the future institutionalization of parliament (Maddicott, 2015, p.24). Similarly, this section discusses how regime changes, rulers' centralization efforts, drastic civil wars, and elite migrations induced the emergence of *Keju* as a contingent solution. The next section details additional forces at play in the following three centuries that retrospectively make 622 CE appear eventful in a reverse Whiggish manner.

2.2.6 An Existing Study

Before moving on, we address an existing economics study that attempts to use 605 CE as the "treatment" year for the emergence of *Keju* (Chen, Fan, and Huang, 2023). The paper analyzes a limited set of biographies from Chinese dynastic histories spanning from 265 to 1644 CE. Its core finding is that after 605 CE, bureaucrats who last served as local administrators were more likely to be purged than those who last served in central ministries. The authors use this result to argue that *Keju* undermined the aristocracy. Our critique underscores a key point: *Keju* did not emerge as a sudden shock but rather as a gradual process, evolving alongside various other developments over an extended period.

We outline four major flaws in the study, with a detailed analysis provided in the Online Appendix. First, the authors misreported the timing of the treatment. They cite Miyazaki (1981) to support 605 CE, despite this source clearly stating that *Keju* began in 587 CE, with no mention of 605 CE in its timeline of institutional changes. Notably, 587 CE falls just before the treatment decade in the authors' event study. Second, as discussed in Section 2.2.4, any form of *Keju* before 622 CE still limited candidacy to those nominated by incumbent elites, likely reinforcing rather than undermining aristocratic dominance. Third, the authors' operationalization of aristocracy is highly unconventional, equating local (central) administrators with "commoners" ("aristocrats"), a view not supported by the historical sources they cite.[36] Lastly, as detailed in the Online Appendix, numerous events and political changes in the decade following 605 CE likely altered the fortunes of both nobility and commoners, further confounding the study's results, but the authors did not disclose these well-known historical facts.

Our critique highlights the *gradual* nature of *Keju*'s emergence, making it impossible to pinpoint a singular "treatment" effect. Historians have identified at least ten different eras for the emergence of *Keju* (Liu, 2000). These ambiguities and controversies arise because *Keju* evolved gradually as an outgrowth of earlier institutions, rather than emerging as a significant, singular event.

3 Early Development

This section explains how *Keju* gradually became the dominant pathway to power despite its minimal and ad hoc beginnings. First, it uses qualitative evidence to show how the aristocrats failed to recognize that *Keju* would eventually promote social mobility, leading to their lack of collective resistance. Specifically, *Keju*'s rise was so gradual that the "signal" of this development was hard to discern from the various noises of politics. Next, it quantitatively

---

[36] Moreover, the study's results actually suggest that the "commoner" group (local administrators) was disproportionately undermined after 605 CE, which could imply that *Keju* weakened nonaristocrats rather than aristocrats as the authors claimed.

confirms the gradual increase in the importance of *Keju*, establishing that it had indeed become significant over time. Finally, it explores the institution's positive feedback (Mahoney, Thelen et al., 2009), in which both rulers and the broader elite came to see *Keju* as beneficial. The rulers gradually realized that *Keju* had the potential to equalize political opportunities and expand the selectorate, while specific political developments in the latter half of the Tang made *Keju* more central to career success for the elites.

3.1 Signal versus Noise: What Happened under Empress Wu?

Thus far, we have demonstrated that *Keju* emerged from a gradual institutional evolution spanning four hundred years. This period witnessed the initial decline and subsequent revival of examinations in bureaucratic recruitment. To the contemporaneous elites, its "inception" – if there was one to speak of – would likely have been perceived not as a revolutionary break, but as a continuation of an ongoing process. However, there is no denying that by the end of the Tang, *Keju* had become a game changer. By the mid-7th century, less than 22% of the Tang chief ministers entered the bureaucracy through *Keju*, but this proportion increased to a stunning 85% for chief ministers in the 9th century. Furthermore, only 3.8% of the male elites had examination credentials by the mid-7th century, but the number increased to 17.6% for male elites in the 9th century.[37]

Given its modest beginnings, what explains *Keju*'s rise over the next three hundred years? A popular theory credits Empress Wu (武则天) in the late 7th century. As the only female monarch in a Confucian society, she faced strong opposition from the aristocracy and is thought to have promoted *Keju* to weaken their influence by introducing new talent into the bureaucracy. This idea, proposed by historian Chen Yinke in the 1940s, has faced significant criticism over the years but has recently been revisited by social scientists like Huang (2023), who argue that *Keju* strengthened autocratic rule.[38]

While several changes under Empress Wu could have elevated *Keju* – such as allowing more people to pass exams, holding exams more frequently, and shifting the exam focus toward literature – there was no significant aristocratic dissent recorded, making this narrative difficult to substantiate. This lack of resistance returns us to our initial puzzle: Why did the aristocracy not resist more? In what follows, we explore this question through a thought experiment.

Unlike the minimal changes in 622 CE, the shifts in *Keju* during Empress Wu's reign may have been significant enough to be noticed. However, political selection is a noisy process, and for the powerholders to react, the signal of what

---

[37] We arrive at these comparisons by analyzing data from Wen, Wang, and Hout (2024).
[38] See Xiang (2012) for a survey of critiques.

The Political Economy of China's Keju System   25

these changes meant for political power needed to be clear. In Tang politics, a clear signal would have been the rising importance of *Keju* in appointing chief ministers, but it's possible that the powerholders struggled to distinguish signal from noise.

Among the 105 individuals who served as chief minister during Empress Wu's era (649–705 CE), 32.11% began their bureaucratic careers through *Keju*.[39] This percentage represents a 50% increase from the era of the dynasty's first two emperors (618–649 CE), a rise that could have been noticeable at the time. The key question, however, is whether these *Keju*-credentialed chief ministers became chief ministers *because of Keju*. This question is not one of "causal identification" in the pedantic sense. It is simply whether the incumbent powerholders at the time intuitively *perceived* that success in *Keju*, a competition with a relatively level playing field even for their own children, was becoming increasingly important for officeholding.[40] The answer is: unlikely.

When someone ascends to a top bureaucratic position after decades of service, many of his traits would have been observed, with passing a written exam decades earlier being just one of them. In this thought experiment, we suggest that discerning the rise of *Keju* as a key factor in appointing a chief minister, amidst other "confounding" factors, would be challenging for a powerholder. Take the example of Di Renjie (狄仁杰), whose administrative competence and moral integrity were widely praised by contemporaries. During his term in the Ministry of Justice, he reportedly resolved 17,000 backlogged cases in one year without any complaints of injustice. He also saved an official from wrongful execution, even daring to openly confront the Emperor Gaozong for this cause. The Emperor later rewarded him for his courage and integrity.[41] It seems unlikely that other elites would attribute his eventual promotion to chief minister to his earlier *Keju* success rather than to his widely recognized qualities. Another example is Wei Siqian (韦思谦). His exemplary county governance early in his career earned significant acclaim. Then as an imperial censor, he was praised for impartiality. He even launched anti-corruption charges against a chief minister, who revenged by demoting him. Several years later, the same chief minister was killed for opposing Wu's promotion to Empress. Wei's

---

[39] 649 marked the start of Emperor Gaozong's reign, during which Wu was made Empress in 655 CE. As Gaozong's health deteriorated, Wu increasingly gained power, becoming regent upon his death in 683 CE, and eventually claiming the throne in 690 CE. Her official reign as the *de jure* emperor lasted until 705 CE.

[40] Wen, Wang, and Hout (2024) suggests that within the broader elite spectrum, family background had limited impact on passing the *Keju* during the Tang dynasty.

[41] *Old Book of Tang*, vol. 89.

career subsequently advanced, attaining important positions. Wei then got promoted again, attaining important positions throughout his career. When Wei became chief minister at the age of seventy-four, it would have been difficult for others to see this as a result of passing the *Keju* four decades prior, rather than his administrative capabilities and a political gamble that eventually paid off.

To systematically document these "noises," we compile original data on recorded qualities. For each of the thirty-five chief ministers with a *Keju* background, we examined their biographies in the *Old Book of Tang* and *New Book of Tang*, assessing whether they were also noted for merits or achievements in areas relevant to high office promotion: morality, literature, military, civil administration, knowledge of rituals, and notable political deeds.[42] Remarkably, 91.4% had merits recorded in at least one of these dimensions. Excluding "literature," a dimension often seen as closely tied to *Keju* success, this percentage still stands at a significant 77.1%. This exercise confirms our idea that the aristocratic powerholders were unlikely to detect the signal of *Keju*'s rising primacy from the "noises" as far as political power was concerned.

The rise of *Keju* continued throughout the era of Empress Wu. While the changes it had brought to political power were noisy enough initially, they had become clearer over time. After dividing Empress Wu's era into earlier (649–689 CE) and later (690–705 CE) periods, we see that the 32.3% of the chief ministers were *Keju*-credentialed in the earlier period, but the number grew to 43.1% in the later period.[43] Following a brief interlude after Wu stepped down in 705 CE, Tang China entered its stablest and most prosperous era under Emperor Xuanzong, which lasted until 755 CE. Between the end of Wu and the end of Xuanzong, this percentage rose to 61.9%. Given that becoming a chief minister was the ultimate aspiration for Tang elites, the majority having ascended through the examination system was a clear indicator of *Keju*'s significance. By the mid-8th century, *Keju* had arguably become the primary route to the highest echelon of political power. Should a time machine have existed, a Tang elite from the mid-7th century traveling forward a century would likely find the politics of bureaucratic recruitment dramatically transformed upon looking back.[44]

---

[42] The first five dimensions were all considered essential qualities for bureaucrats in medieval China. Notable political deeds include both acts that demonstrate high political integrity (such as defiance of higher officials or emperors when they made moves seen as detrimental to the realm) and successful power politics maneuvers.

[43] 690 is the year when Empress Wu officially declared herself to be an emperor and founded the Zhou dynasty.

[44] The analysis here assumes that the proportion of *Keju*-credentialed bureaucrats in high offices acted as a signal to the broader elite. Once this proportion reached a certain threshold, *Keju*

3.1.1 What the Data Says

Now we illustrate the gradual yet significant rise of *Keju* throughout the Tang dynasty with more systematic data. Our analysis is based on career data from 3,640 *epitaphs* of adult males from the Tang period, drawn from Wen, Wang, and Hout (2024).[45] Unlike biographies from dynastic histories that predominantly feature high-ranking elites and political "winners," epitaphic data is widely acknowledged by historians of medieval China as providing a more representative sample of the broader Tang elite society (e.g. Jiang, 2006, 2012; Tackett, 2014, 2020).[46] We use the following specification:

$$\text{Rank}_{iprt} = \Sigma_k \alpha_k \mathbf{X}_{ki} + \Sigma_k \beta_k \mathbf{X}_{ki} \times T + \Sigma_k \gamma_k \mathbf{X}_{ki} \times T^2 + \mu_{pt} + \xi_{rt} + \epsilon_{iprt}.$$

The level of analysis is individual, the deceased person for whom the epitaph was written. The outcome is the rank of the last office obtained in his career, which takes zero if he had not been in the bureaucracy. $\mathbf{X}$ denotes k number of independent variables, including whether he had passed the *Keju*, the rank of the highest office taken by his father, the rank of the highest office taken by his grandfather, whether he belonged to a prominent aristocratic branch, and whether he belonged to the elite marriage network based in the two capitals of the Tang dynasty (Tackett, 2020).[47] This specification therefore follows Wen, Wang, and Hout (2024) to decompose "medieval aristocracy" into two dimensions. One is the power of the individual's immediate ancestors, measured by the office ranks of the father and grandfather. Another is the *pedigree*

---

would have appeared to be the game in town for them. This assumption aligns with Tang contemporaries' sentiments. A late-8th-century historian, who was a bureaucrat himself, suggested that Empress Wu made essay-writing skills demonstrated via *Keju* exams central to political success. According to his commentary, over the next century, officials increasingly advanced through such skills, signaling to all levels of society, even down to "boys of five feet tall," to hone their writing abilities in preparation of *Keju* exams. This interpretation supports our analysis, reflecting a consistent trajectory of *Keju*'s growing influence. The commentary is drawn from Volume 15 of *Comprehensive Statutes*. Despite potential recollection bias, the historian's family's multi-generational service in the Tang bureaucracy lends credibility to his account.

[45] The epitaphs utilized in Wen, Wang, and Hout (2024) are catalogued by Tackett (2020). However, the catalogue in Tackett (2020) does not provide the original text of the epitaphs, information on the office ranks of the individuals and their family members, or their *Keju* achievements. Consequently, Wen, Wang, and Hout (2024) independently collected this information for each epitaph used.

[46] The appendix of Wen, Wang, and Hout (2024) includes various sensitivity tests demonstrating that potential sample selection biases do not significantly alter the conclusions about *Keju* drawn from the data.

[47] This variable is the definition of "aristocracy" in Tackett (2014) and Tackett (2020).

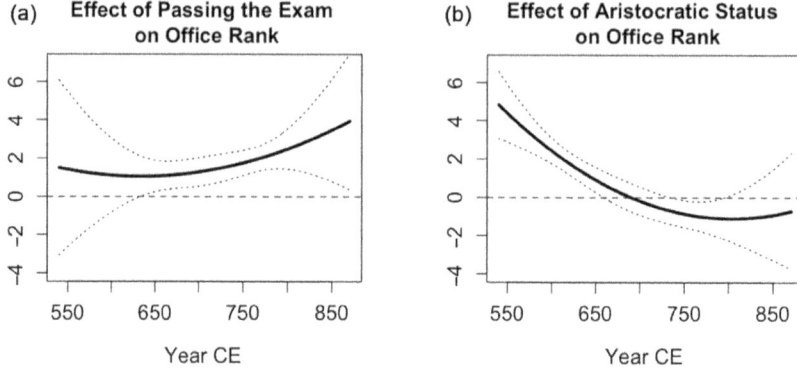

Figure 2 Panel (a) shows the effect over time of passing the *Keju* on one's office rank. Panel (b) shows the effect over time of being a member of a prominent aristocratic branch on one's office rank. Both are with 95% confidence intervals.

of the bloodline itself, proxied with membership in a prominent branch of a choronym-surname.[48]

The person's decade of birth is denoted by t, which we refer to as "time." We evaluate the effects of these variables, *Keju* in particular, on the individual's political achievement over time by including the interaction between them and the square and cubic terms of birth year with T and T^2. The province-time fixed effects are denoted by μ_{pt}, where p denotes the modern province in which the epitaph was excavated, and ξ_{rt} is the interaction between time dummies and ancestral regime dummies. As China was divided into three regimes in the northwest, northeast, and south before unification under the Sui-Tang empire, elites serving in the Sui and Tang Dynasties might belong to different factions based on the geopolitical identities of the regime their family descended from.[49]

Figure 2(a) shows that the significance of *Keju* success as a predictor of an elite's political achievement increased over the course of the dynasty. Initially, its predictive power for office rank was indistinguishable from zero. However, the lower bound of the confidence intervals went above zero for cohorts whose political coming-of-age coincided with the initial ascendancy of Empress Wu. Since then, the significance of *Keju* had continued to grow. For cohorts active in

---

[48] Medieval Chinese aristocrats were initially identified through choronym-surname combinations (e.g. Ebrey, 1978; Chen, Wang, and Zhang, 2025), but the choronym-based identities became no longer distinguishable for various reasons in the Tang. Aristocrats adopted branch status as a more specific identity marker. See Wen, Wang, and Hout (2024) and its appendix for detailed discussions.

[49] For example, one ancestral regime dummy takes 1 if an elite's family had served in the northwestern Yuwen regime. This identity forms the core of what Chen (1982) referred to as the "Guanlong Block," hypothesized to play a prominent role in early Tang politics.

the late Tang, passing the *Keju* could translate into a career advantage of two full ranks within the bureaucracy's nine-rank system.[50] The continuously increasing trend of *Keju*'s importance, gradual but substantial, is consistent with our qualitative analysis at the beginning of this section.

We now explore the association between aristocratic status and political success, where two key observations emerge from the right panel. First, the significance of belonging to a prominent aristocratic branch for securing office positions declined throughout the Tang dynasty. By the generation born in the mid-7th century, aristocratic status ceased to be a reliable predictor of career success. Because whether an individual could be credibly traced to a prominent aristocratic branch is technically measured "before" his father and grandfather office ranks, his status in the marriage networks, and his success in the *Keju*, X in the specification excludes such control variables.[51] Second, this downward trend in the value of aristocratic lineage *predated* the rise in importance of *Keju*, as evidenced in the left panel. This contrast further casts doubt on the grand narrative critiqued throughout this Element that early Tang *Keju* aimed to undermine the "aristocracy."

The empirical results here, alongside Wen, Wang, and Hout (2024), challenge the recent "persistent school" in Tang studies, which downplays the significance of *Keju* and overemphasizes the enduring influence of aristocratic advantage in officeholding (e.g. Tackett, 2014, 2020).[52]

This does not imply that family background was inconsequential. In fact, findings in Wen, Wang, and Hout (2024) indicate that the office ranks of both fathers and grandfathers had a positive impact on the office rank of sons, with these trends remaining stable over time (neither increasing nor decreasing). Given that the significance of immediate ancestors in an individual's success is a universal phenomenon across various cultures and eras, its consistent importance in the Tang dynasty is hardly surprising.[53] By comparing the steady influence of immediate ancestors' ranks with the declining significance of

---

[50] This "nine-rank" system is not to be confused with the NRRS. Here, "rank" denotes the numeric level assigned to specific offices in the Tang bureaucracy, reflecting their importance and salary. The outcome variable in the analysis ranges from 0 to 17.75, accommodating sub-ranks within a full rank. For more details, see Section 1A of the appendix in Wen, Wang, and Hout (2024).

[51] The declining trend is even sharper with these controls included (Wen, Wang, and Hout, 2024).

[52] Although similar epitaphic data are used, the persistent school does not employ regression analysis, relying instead on descriptive statistics that "select on the dependent variable." See Wang (2024) for a more direct critique.

[53] The father-to-son mobility correlation, in the simplest specification, is 0.41. As noted in Wen, Wang, and Hout (2024), this magnitude is lower than for men in 19th-century Europe but comparable to men in contemporary United States.

broader ancestral prestige, it can be argued that in the era of examinations, the bureaucracy in medieval China became less "medieval" and aristocratic.

What about the effect of family background on examination success? A prevailing notion in the literature on *Keju* during the Tang dynasty states that the overwhelming majority of *Keju* passers (those who succeeded in the exam) were themselves "aristocrats" (Sun, 1980; Mao, 1988; Kung, 2022). This statistical claim is problematic on multiple levels. First, a complete government roster of *Keju* passers (those who succeeded in the exam) from the Tang dynasty was never preserved. Any effort by post-Tang historians to compile a complete "list" of Tang *Keju* passers has had to either rely on reading biographies from dynastic histories, a sample that is severely biased for various reasons (e.g. Jiang, 2006, 2012; Tackett, 2014, 2020), or rely on secondary "catalogues" (e.g. *Dengke Jikao* 《登科记考》), which in turn relied heavily on dynastic histories.[54] When historians compute the proportion of aristocrats in any such "list," those outside the list and those inside the list but without detailed family information are essentially omitted from the denominator, leading to upward bias in favor of aristocratic dominance as prestigious family backgrounds were more likely to be recorded in history.[55]

Second, works claiming that the overmajority of *Keju* passers were aristocrats employ definitions of "aristocrats" that not only are excessively expansive but also fundamentally deviate from the Tang reality. Their definitions rely solely (as in Kung, 2022) or significantly (as in Sun, 1980 and Mao, 1988) on "choronym-surname" combinations ("choronym" meaning an elite's ancestral hometown).[56] There is overwhelming consensus among historians that the fabrication or "concoction" (建构郡望) of choronyms was *widespread* in the Tang (e.g. Qiu, 2016; Fan, 2014).[57] Anyone with surname Li, an extremely

---

[54] *Dengke Jikao* also collected other names from nonstandard sources that rarely provide info on the candidate's family background, other than the place of origin. Using just surname and place of origin (often thought to be "choronym") to identify aristocrat is problematic. See our discussion next.

[55] Reliable information exists to compute the total number of individuals who passed the exam. According to the authors' calculations based on the tabulation in Jin (2015), for the *Jinshi* exam (the most prestigious and challenging category of the *Keju*) alone, there were already 6,585 candidates certified as passing it. However, as of 2015, scholars had been able to reconstruct the names and exam years of only 1,586 of these individuals based on traces left in historical records, and even fewer had detailed information about their family backgrounds. A striking example of drawing inference from severely incomplete lists is Sun (1980), which calculates the proportion of aristocrats based on a list of only 301 individuals (even though the actual denominator could exceed 6,585). This led to an estimate of 76% for P(Aristocrat|Keju Success), later referenced in Kung (2022), where the estimate is rounded to 80%.

[56] The method of measuring aristocrats in Kung (2022) can be found in Chen and Kung (2009).

[57] Due to waves of nationwide migrations in medieval China, many aristocrats themselves in the Tang were also mistaken about their choronyms, leading to fabrication of choronyms among

common surname in Chinese history and today, could claim to come originally from the choronym Longxi or Zhaojun and enter the data in these works as a member of the aristocratic clan "Li of Longxi" (陇西李氏) or "Li of Zhaojun" (赵郡李氏).[58] In addition to these two major problems, the methodology of computing $P(Aristocrat|Keju\ Success)$ from any "list" of *Keju* passers is itself inherently flawed as it selects on the dependent variable.

The more adequate approach would be to obtain a *sample* of Tang elites, which would inevitably contain individuals with *Keju* credential and individuals without it, and employ a precise definition of aristocrats that reduces the fabrication bias inherent in choronym-based measures that has been well-documented in the historical literature. The epitaph sample and the methodology of measuring the *pedigree* dimension of medieval Chinese aristocracy in Wen, Wang, and Hout (2024) underpins this approach. Our simple calculation suggests that only 38% of the *Keju* passers in the epitaph sample could be credibly traced to prominent aristocratic branches, much lower than prior estimates.[59]

More importantly, econometric analyses by Wen, Wang, and Hout (2024) suggest that none of the family background measures consistently predicts exam success, whether they are father or grandfather office ranks, membership in elite marriage networks based in the Tang capitals (a measure

---

aristocrats. For example, "Wang" has always been a prevalent surname in China, and there were two choronym–surname combinations involving Wang that were thought to be aristocratic clans centuries prior to the Tang: Wang of Taiyuan (太原王氏) and Wang of Langya (琅琊王氏). Hilariously, during the Tang dynasty, some members of both clans mistakenly believed they were low-born and fabricated their lineage as belonging to the other clan in an attempt to reclaim aristocratic status, having completely forgotten their true ancestral roots (Fan, 2014).

[58] A related problem is that if a *Keju* passer was truly born and raised in a Tang prefecture that was once the choronym of a prominent aristocratic clan with the same surname, his own residence in that prefecture could only suggest that he was *not* from a privileged class. After all, aristocratic clans had already relocated to Tang's capital regions for generations (Section 2.2.5; Ebrey, 1978; Tackett, 2020), so this individual was at most distant descendant whose ancestors got left behind for several centuries. Why would one think someone with surname "Washington" in Tyne and Wear, England (a place where the ancestors of George Washington stayed until the 14th century) would be a member of the political elite in 19th-century United States?

[59] Another measure of aristocracy immune to the fabrication bias is constructed in Tackett (2014, 2020), which defines someone as aristocratic if he belonged to the elite marriage networks based in Tang's capitals. Calculation using this metric yields 52.5%. However, this alternative definition suffers from a "post-treatment" bias that inherently causes overestimation of aristocrats' proportion. Anyone from a humble background who hailed from *Keju* and married *into* this elite network would enter the data as an "aristocrat." Prominent chief ministers such as Miao Jinqing (苗晋卿) and Niu Sengru (牛僧孺) epitomized such rags-to-riches stories enabled by *Keju* success. They were initially outsiders to the network as their fathers, grandfathers, and even great grandfathers were never politically notable. They attained high positions after passing *Keju* and married into this network.

of aristocracy preferred by Tackett (2014)), or membership in a prominent aristocratic branch.⁶⁰ These nonresults should not be misconstrued to suggest that the *Keju* contest was entirely equitable across all societal classes or groups. The epitaph sample primarily reflects the *elite* segment of Tang society – individuals who were highly educated and could afford epitaphs. However, these nonresults in Wen, Wang, and Hout (2024), along with the concurrent trends of increasing *Keju* importance and diminishing aristocratic influence reported in Figure 2, support our argument in Section 1 that *Keju* broadened the "selectorate" by leveling the playing field *within* the elite class. The remainder of this section will explore how *Keju* evolved into a self-enforcing institution perceived as beneficial by both the emperor and (to some extent) elites, where we will further illustrate the equalizing nature of the Tang *Keju* through additional qualitative and quantitative evidence.

3.2 Self-reinforcing Institution

We now move to the next question: Why did *Keju* become an institution that sustains itself. Our answer is that both the ruler and the elites increasingly found it beneficial. For the ruler, although we initially minimized the notion that *Keju* was intentionally implemented to weaken the aristocracy or existing political powerholders, from a certain point onward, it became increasingly clear to the Tang emperors themselves that *Keju* indeed could serve such a political purpose. For the elites, they adapted to the new paradigm and began to view the *Keju*-credential as a key step in their political promotion. Our discussion starts with the perspective of the ruler.

3.2.1 The Equalizing Potential of Keju

Even in the subsection discussing Empress Wu, whom some historians and social scientists view as a crucial advocate of *Keju* with the aim of undermining the upper elites, we remain agnostic regarding her actual intentions, emphasizing instead the incremental and "noisy" evolution of *Keju* and consequently the absence of elite resistance. Nonetheless, it prompts the question of when Tang emperors eventually began to recognize *Keju*'s potential to serve the purpose often attributed to it: enhancing the ruler's power. While it is impossible to look inside a ruler's mind, we consider the increasing attention to a specific political issue as indirect evidence of Tang emperors acknowledging *Keju* as a tool to

---

[60] In certain specifications, membership in elite marriage networks became mildly predictive of exam success in the second half of the 9th century, but this small advantage did not translate into an advantage in officeholding. See the appendix of Wen, Wang, and Hout (2024).

broaden the "selectorate." This issue pertains to the participation of *zidi* (子弟) in the exam.

Zidi (子弟): children of powerful political families. The term *zidi* literally translates to "young offspring," but within the Tang dynasty's context, it specifically denotes the descendants and nephews of high-ranking officials, up to two generations (e.g. Lu, 2016). In the Tang system, officials ranked five or higher would have a limited number of their offspring automatically entitled to certain entry-level bureaucratic positions (a system known as *men-yin* 门荫). However, the majority of *zidi* were ineligible for these positions and thus competed in the *Keju* for bureaucratic entry. Notably, as the importance of *Keju* for officeholding grew over time, even those *zidi* who qualified for automatic entry increasingly opted to partake in the *Keju*. Needless to say, *zidi* were perceived to have an inherently unfair advantage because of their familial ties. Imperial court discussions regarding the entry of *zidi* into the bureaucracy via the *Keju* were predominantly negative. Such pronounced worries about *zidi*'s participation in the *Keju* clearly indicate the emperor's concern for maintaining fairness in the competition. The rulers' attention to and efforts in preserving the "equalizing" aspect of the *Keju* should, in turn, be seen as evidence that they had indeed recognized its potential to broaden political access across a wider spectrum.

The earliest mention of the *zidi* issue in the historical records referred to the demotion of a *Keju* examiner in 789 CE. The emperor punished him specifically for "awarding many degrees to the *zidi* of high-ranking and influential officials."[61] Contrast this incident and its historical description with the anecdote in Section 2.2.4, which illuminates the early Tang dynasty's more favorable view of a similar phenomenon. In the case of Zhang Chujin, facilitated by Xu Shiji's intervention, the narrative positively portrays the selection of officials' children through the *Keju* system. This account signifies a time when such practices were not only exempt from punishment but were also celebrated as a means of recognizing and advancing genuine talent. This stark contrast marked a notable shift in the approach to merit and influence within the imperial examination system. Notably, the word *zidi* wasn't even used in the historical records describing phenomena of patronage in the early Tang *Keju*. It was in the 9th century, however, that the issue of *zidi* truly intensified, notably during the so-called Niu-Li Factional Strife (牛李党争) and its aftermath. We now turn to this important episode in the development of *Keju*, an episode as fascinating as it is misunderstood.

---

[61] *New Book of Tang*, vol. 203.

Affirmative Actions in the *Keju*

In 846 CE, the governor of Xuanshe Province received a letter from his friend, Du Mu (杜牧), one of the most renowned poets in Chinese history. Enclosed was a vehement political critique, disguised as an argumentative essay, targeting a chief minister in the Tang court.[62] The essay opens with:

> Since five years ago, those in charge have proposed that the selection of bureaucrats through *Keju* examinations should be reserved for scholars from humble backgrounds, and that *zidi* should not be advanced this way. This idea has become ingrained in the Emperor's mind, firmly held in his heart, and implemented rigorously, as unyielding as metal and stone. Consequently, *zidi* find themselves hiding like fish in deep waters or mice in burrows, with no path to enter the bureaucracy. This perplexes me.

Du Mu was someone who "checked all the boxes." A descendant of a distinguished ancient house from the Tang capital, Chang'an, Du Mu boasted of his grandfather's notable tenure as a chief minister. Additionally, one of his elder cousins was a son-in-law of Emperor Xianzong. In 828 CE, Du Mu excelled in the *Keju* exam at the age of twenty-five as a *zidi*, achieving fifth place. He then went on to succeed in a special *Keju* test, securing expedited entry into officialdom.[63] Yet, at the time of writing this letter, Du Mu had only six years remaining in his life and had not yet secured any significant position within the central government.[64] The remainder of his essay voices a passionate outcry against the discrimination toward *zidi* highlighted at the outset, so intense that a keen reader couldn't help but speculate that Du Mu attributed his own career underplacement to this policy.

> "The very point of *Keju*, as envisioned by our enlightened founding emperors, was to recruit talents irrespective of family background, be it humble or noble. In ancient times, when in urgent need, rulers would recruit talents from all walks of life, including thieves, enemies, or even barbarians. How illogical then, that we employ *Keju* to identify talent, yet exclude *zidi* from selection?"

---

[62] *Complete Prose of the Tang*, vol. 752.

[63] This test, known as the "decree examination" (制举), was for individuals unwilling to endure the potentially lengthy wait between passing the *Keju* and starting their bureaucratic careers. This additional exam, offered less frequently, provided a faster path.

[64] For an overview of Du Mu's career history and the relative significance of the offices he pursued, refer to Lai (2011, pp. 159–162). Du Mu eventually became an Edict Drafter with a formal office rank of "five plus" at the age of forty-eight, passing away a year later. Section 3.2.2 discusses the growing importance of the Edict Drafter role in Tang politics. However, Du attained this role at a relatively advanced age. The chief minister critiqued in his essay, for example, became an Edict Drafter at the age of thirty-five, without ever passing the *Keju*. Or consider Bai Juyi (白居易), Du's rival in poetry who came from a significantly humbler family. Bai also became a Edict Drafter at the age of thirty-five.

Du Mu fervently argued. He proceeded to enumerate a total of *seventy* ancient figures who not only had significant political achievements but also came from privileged backgrounds. He then highlighted that in more recent history, "countless" descendants from high-ranking officials have been recognized as great figures. "Why then, would we assume that *zidi* cannot be talented today?" He lamented.

The essay then drifts to a defense of *Keju* itself, countering claims that those chosen through the exam were "frivolous" (浮华) and untalented. Du enumerated *nineteen* distinguished historical figures from the Tang dynasty with *Keju* credentials. "All these nineteen esteemed individuals have made significant contributions to the state's well-being. What, then, is the issue with *Keju*?" Du Mu asked in despair. The essay concludes with commendation for the provincial governor's third son, who had reached adulthood. Du Mu lauded the son's exceptional essays, noting that had this son participated in the *Keju* five or six years earlier, he would by now be serving as an esteemed official in the central government. Yet, Du expressed regret that the recent anti-*zidi* stance had imposed significant obstacles. "The vetting in the *Keju* has become akin to laying nets and traps, as if warding off thieves. *Zidi* suffer in silence, burdened and disheartened, longing to discard their noble attire and join the lower class, facing a deadlock so bizarre and unprecedented in both ancient and modern times," Du Mu mourned in depression.

The profound frustration and despair conveyed in Du's essay starkly highlight the anti-*zidi* sentiment in the Tang court during his lifetime. The chief minister anonymously criticized in Du's piece is Li Deyu (李德裕), the "Li" in the so-called Niu-Li Factional Strife. Li came from an even more illustrious lineage than Du's. He clashed with another influential official, Niu Sengru (牛僧孺), over policies and personal issues, leading to a broader rivalry involving allies of Niu and Li, marked by accusations of factionalism.

Historian Chen Yinke boldly argued that the Niu-Li Strife was rooted in differing views on the *Keju*: Li's faction opposed it, representing aristocrats whose status was threatened, while Niu's faction supported it, representing new elites from modest backgrounds. Chen's thesis was refuted in 1950 by another historian who found no significant differences in either *Keju* credentials or family backgrounds between the two factions (Cen, 2020). This rebuttal was then supported and enriched by scholars in Japan and the United States.[65] Later historians have even questioned the existence of distinct factions (Wang, 2018; Fu, 2023).

---

[65] See Dalby (1979) for a summary.

The consensus since the 1980s has underscored that Li Deyu, though a *zidi* of noble lineage himself, notably strongly favored promoting individuals from *humble* backgrounds into the bureaucracy via *Keju*, rather than *zidi*. In contrast, his adversaries sought to support the advancement of each other's children as *zidi* to the highest ranks of political power (e.g. Wang, 2018; Fu, 2023). Li's stance on the *Keju* is another source of confusion. Despite the availability of automatic entry into the bureaucracy for *zidi* like himself and his father through the *men-yin* system, many ambitious *zidi* opted for the *Keju*, believing that having such credentials could help them in their careers. However, Li and his father abstained from the *Keju*, influenced by their family's deep respect for ancient rituals and Confucian classics, which led them to critique the shift toward lavish literary expression in the *Keju* (Chen, 1982). Ironically, Li's own literary talents, particularly in styles crucial for *Keju* success, were widely admired among the elite (Lu, 2016). Nevertheless, he frequently rebuked *Keju*'s overemphasis on literary skills and criticized the *Jinshi* degree holders as "frivolous" (a point raised in Du's essay). Li's cultural and familial background created the *misunderstanding* that he opposed *Keju* out of a desire for aristocrats to retain political power (Wang, 2018). In truth, Li enacted policies to *reform* the *Keju*, reducing corruption and preventing other powerful officials from co-opting the institution as a means of elite reproduction. Li envisioned it instead as a pathway for elites from humbler background to join the bureaucracy (Wang, 2018; Fu, 2020; Fu, 2023).

While we agree with the historians' "rehabilitation" of Li Deyu, the literature misses the bigger picture. It's the Tang emperors, not just Li, who had consistently taken actions to preserve the equalizing potential of the *Keju*. The anti-*zidi* policies were not Li's alone. Tang chief ministers rarely acted independently of the emperor, as their positions were ultimately at the emperor's discretion, who could dismiss them for deviating from his will. There were 364 chief ministers in total, with an average of 6.248 chief ministers serving an emperor in any given year, and the average tenure was only 2.157 years. Li's continuous role as chief minister throughout Emperor Wuzong's full six-year reign was an exception. Annually, there were about 3.667 colleagues serving as chief ministers alongside Li, each with an average tenure of 1.875 years. Emperor Wuzong saw Li as a loyalist whose anti-*zidi* stance aligned with his own ambition of unleashing *Keju*'s equalizing potential. The Emperor once noted, "the examiners didn't fully grasp the true intention (of affirmative action). Not letting any *zidi* pass the exam is a bit too extreme. The point is to select talents without bias towards the low-born or *zidi*." Li adeptly aligned with his Emperor in the conversation, smoothly picking up on the Emperor's cues, by replying that *zidi* were also useful for the empire.⁶⁶ This exchange underscores that the emperor was the principal architect of the policy, which was enacted to such an extent that he felt compelled to moderate it.

These policies were not exclusive to Wuzong's reign, either. The first recorded instance of such actions dates back to 789 CE, as previously noted. Throughout the 9th century, efforts to curtail *zidi*'s edge in the *Keju* unfolded to varying degrees under every emperor except one.⁶⁷ In the 9th century, it was common for a newly announced list of *Keju* passers to be scrutinized by the emperor, who, upon noticing numerous sons and relatives of high-ranking officials among the passers, would command the examiners to explicitly remove some of them from the list ("令落下"). Similarly, if public outcry arose over the presence of *zidi* on a publicly announced list, the emperor would mandate a "re-test" ("覆试"), leading to the revocation of some *zidi*'s degrees as a result.⁶⁸ These efforts also continued beyond the Tang. In 985 CE, Emperor Taizong (宋太宗) of the Song dynasty (960–1279 CE), upon noticing the cousins and sons of three senior officials from the degree list, famously said: "These were all from powerful families. Even if they passed the exam with true talent, people would think that I am playing favors!" He revoked all their degrees afterwards.⁶⁹ It seems that Tang and early Song rulers were less concerned with procedural fairness itself than with ensuring equality of outcomes. Measures under Emperor Wuzong were particularly harsh, as they were not merely about "leveling" the playing field between privileged and underprivileged groups; they actively discriminated against the privileged, even to the extent of barring them from passing the *Keju* (Wu, 1992, chapter 12). For Wuzong and Li, given that well-connected officials had numerous methods to secure political power for their *zidi* at the expense of social mobility, simple equality of opportunity was deemed insufficient for achieving true equality of outcomes. They had to take more drastic actions.

---

⁶⁶ *Old Book of Tang*, vol. 18.
⁶⁷ The sole exception was Wuzong's uncle and immediate successor, who, amidst complex and intense family feuds, chose to signal a wholesale departure from Wuzong's policies and harshly penalized any official loyal to Wuzong. Li Deyu and his associates were wiped out. For an in-depth discussion, refer to the appendix of Wang (2018).
⁶⁸ See chapter 11 of Wu (1992) for an analysis, although Li Deyu himself was misunderstood as pro-*zidi* there.
⁶⁹ *Extended Continuation of the Comprehensive Mirrors*, vol. 26. See Chen (2017) for a discussion of the various institutional reforms that made the Song dynasty *Keju* a fairer competition, and political and economic developments that reduced the incentives of the scion of powerful families to compete for offices.

The Broader Context in Data

Our qualitative analysis aligns with the quantitative discussion in Section 3.1.1, where Wen, Wang, and Hout (2024) reports scant evidence for the association between father or grandfather ranks and the likelihood of sons passing the *Keju*. This subsection digs further into *Keju*'s equalizing potential. Our analysis is "inspired" by a logical shift in Du Mu's critique of Li Deyu for barring *zidi* from the *Keju*. Recall that the essay devotes a long paragraph to proving through numerous examples that *zidi* could also be great statesmen. The conclusion speaks again on the difficulties facing *zidi* as the door of *Keju* was being shut to them. Yet, the essay also accuses Li of undervaluing those who had already obtained *Keju* degrees, and defends the *Keju* by enumerating the respected Tang politicians that *Keju* produced. This part of the essay seems to shift the concern from *zidi* attempting the *Keju* to those (*zidi* or non-*zidi*) who have succeeded. It implies that Du perceived general career obstacles for *Keju* passers under Wuzong and Li. Notably, Du was not the only one who had made such an accusation against Li.[70] Modern historians have largely debunked these accusations as factional vendettas, showing Li was in fact celebrated by those from modest backgrounds aiming for officialdom through the *Keju* (e.g. Wang, 2018; Fu, 2020; Fu, 2023). Our quantitative evidence in Figure 2 further disproves these accusations, demonstrating the growing value of a *Keju* degree over time in the Tang.

These discrepancies between assertions and reality leads us to speculate that perhaps the accusations weren't about Li Deyu's general aversion to *Keju* passers, but rather his specific disfavor toward *Keju* passers who were *zidi*. Considering Tang rulers' deep concern about equality of outcomes, it's plausible that they also tried leveling the playing field for elites *beyond the examination stage*. In other words, there might have been actions to curtail the advantages *zidi* had over others even after the examination stage. The likes of Du Mu, with the dual-identity of *Keju* passers and *zidi*, could feel underplaced given their distinguished family background, leading to their perception that performance on the exam did not improve their careers.[71] In what follows, we quantitatively demonstrate that Du Mu's frustration as a *zidi* who passed the *Keju* reflects the broader context of *Keju*'s equalizing potential, or efforts to preserve such potential, beyond a particular ruler and chief minister.

---

[70] See *New Book of Tang*, vol. 163, for another example.

[71] There is no doubt another possibility. By preventing *zidi* from *Keju* success, Li inevitably had antagonized numerous powerful families already. It's conceivable that these families had motives to expand their attack on Li, framing Li's anti-*zidi* stance as an issue with *Keju* in general. Such a tactic might gain traction because Li had indeed voiced legitimate concerns regarding *Keju*'s excessive focus on ornate literature, seeking to reform it.

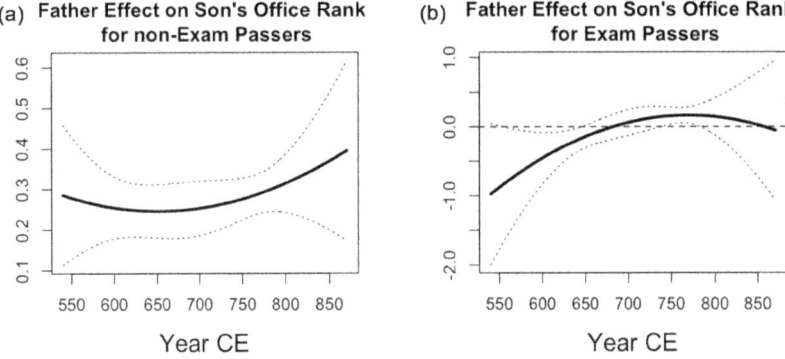

Figure 3 Panel (a) shows the effect over time of father's office rank on son's office rank for non-Exam passers. Panel (b) shows the effect for Exam passers. Both are with 95 % confidence intervals.

Following the sociologists' approach in studying the equalizing effect of education (e.g. Torche, 2011; Hout, 2012), we divide our epitaph sample into sons with *Keju*-credential and sons without, and then conduct the analysis using the specification in Section 3.1. Figure 3(a) shows a consistent association between father office rank and son office rank for non-Exam passers, and the magnitude seems to trend upwards in the 9th century, signaling the rise of *zidi*. Yet, for those who passed the *Keju*, the association between father position and son's career success, as measured by office ranks, is not statistically distinguishable from zero throughout the dynasty. Within the broader elite society, conditional on passing the *Keju*, family background no longer mattered. These results provide a macro-level backdrop against which one could understand the frustration of Du Mu and many others. They also support our overarching argument that *Keju* was a platform through which rulers equalized within the broader elite, keeping the "selectorate" relatively large. Importantly, the discussions and actions toward preserving the equalizing effect of *Keju* in light of the quantitative results showing that it was having an equalizing effect suggest that the emperors by the 9th century had fully understood the political functions of *Keju* that were not so obvious two centuries earlier.

3.2.2 New Political Developments Affecting Elite Incentives

We now turn to the elite perspective, examining the political developments in the latter half of the Tang that further amplified and entrenched *Keju*'s appeal among the Tang elites. There were two interconnected transformations after 755 CE that made *Keju* all the more important for their careers.

Provincial Military Commissioner

The first is the militarization and secessionism of the provinces. For a long time, Tang rulers actively pursued and maintained hegemonic status over East Asia and central Eurasia. To do so, the emperors delegated substantial power to the "provincial military commissioners" (节度使) along its western and eastern borders, who controlled the majority of the imperial armies. In 755 CE, one commissioner named An Lushan launched one of the biggest rebellions in Chinese history, a massive civil war that the dynasty barely survived. In the process of defeating the rebels, the emperors had to allow military generals and local officials across China to raise their own troops. As these generals and officials amassed military power, they increasingly asserted their autonomy. In response, the Tang court formally recognized their elevated status by appointing them as military commissioners to take charge of the inland provinces. A key aftermath of the civil war is therefore the proliferation of semi-autonomous military commissioners not just along the empire's borders but across the Chinese hinterland.

Via a series of war, diplomacy, political maneuvers, and centralization reforms, the Tang rulers eventually reasserted central control over the provinces and were able to appoint, demote, and rotate commissioners at will (Chen and Wang, 2024). To restore loyalty in the provinces, historians note that emperors throughout the 9th century often appointed civilian officials as provincial military commissioners, as they were viewed as more loyal (Qiu, 2018). It's plausible that possessing a *Keju* credential was a crucial factor for appointment as a commissioner, as it demonstrated a vested interest in the central government's strength and the empire's unity. The dedication of time, energy, and resources to master literature and the classics, and to prepare for the exam, signified a family's investment in the dynasty's future. Thus, having passed the *Keju* exam was a signal of a family's loyalty to, and integration within, the Tang political system, distinguishing them from secessionist forces. These provincial commissioner positions were both powerful and lucrative, making them highly coveted by the elite. Equally importantly, governing a province enhanced one's prospects of attaining the position of chief minister. The posts were among the most prestigious and powerful roles available, surpassed only by the chief minister. In short, in the eyes of the elites, a natural path from *Keju* to the provinces, and eventually to the top job in the bureaucracy, had become clear by the 9th century.[72]

---

[72] Admittedly, there were also cases where one became a provincial commissioner after serving as a chief minister.

Hanlin Academian

The second is the position of "Hanlin Academian" (翰林学士) as a pathway from *Keju* to chief minister (McMullen, 1988; Lu, 2016). These academians originated from the Edict Drafting system within the Tang bureaucracy, where the drafting of edicts was integral to all actions taken by the central government. Beginning in the early 8th century, select edict drafters who garnered the emperor's favor were relocated to a new workspace, closer to the emperor's daily activities, dubbed the "Hanlin Academy." This move facilitated the development of close and personal relationships with the emperor. Their daily interactions with the emperor allowed him to micro-manage policy details, bypassing the often cumbersome bureaucratic procedures. Initially, this setup was in a nascent stage, and the Academy's utilization was irregular. Nonetheless, by the late 8th and early 9th centuries, the system had become fully institutionalized, marking a significant evolution in its role and influence. Following the An Lushan Rebellion of 755 CE, the dynasty confronted unparalleled challenges in finance, local governance, and military affairs. Additionally, the upheaval from the Rebellion and subsequent civil wars disrupted the court system itself, occasionally forcing emperors to make crucial policy and political decisions while away from the capital. These unprecedented circumstances compelled the Tang rulers to circumvent the formalities and procedures of their sophisticated, rule-based bureaucracy for the sake of timely decision-making. Consequently, this desire facilitated the rise of the Hanlin academians, primarily serving as edict drafters within the emperor's *inner court*.[73]

As the academians worked closely with the emperor and developed personal relationships with him, their careers often advanced rapidly, frequently culminating in promotion to chief minister. Recent historical research highlights another dimension that further solidified the significance of the Hanlin academians in Tang politics. In the aftermath of the Rebellion of 755 CE, as the Tang court struggled with maintaining the level of centralized control over its territories it once had, it increasingly leveraged soft power. This approach involved the extravagant display of authority through literature to sustain legitimacy among its subjects. Edicts and other documents crafted by the emperor's close associates acted as subtle instruments of propaganda (Lu, 2016; Qiu, 2018). These exogenous developments collectively elevated the Hanlin

---

[73] There is a rich historical consensus regarding the institutional elevation of Hanlin academians as a direct response to the rulers' need for expedited policymaking after the political landscape transformation post-755 CE rebellion. This insight was initially observed by Tang contemporaries (*New Book of Tang*, vol. 43). For recent discussions, see Lu (2016). The term *inner court* contrasts with the regular bureaucracy, including chief ministers, which constituted the *outer court*.

academians to the most distinguished cadre of officials within the bureaucracy, often seen as the stepping stone to becoming chief minister. Hence, the Hanlin Academy came to be known as the "reserve for Chief Ministers" (Lu, 2016, p. 113). The task of edict drafting demanded exceptional writing abilities, particularly in parallel prose, making *Keju* passers, who were rigorously tested on their literary skills during the Tang, prime candidates for the role.

We augment the qualitative discussion with quantitative analyses within the causal mediation framework (Imai et al., 2011), assessing the extent to which *Keju*'s influence on an individual's likelihood of becoming chief minister is mediated by its role in facilitating the individual's appointment as a Hanlin academian or provincial military commissioner. However, due to the stringent assumptions required for causal mediation analysis – particularly when involving two mediators – our findings should be considered indicative of associations rather than causal relationships. Nonetheless, identifying a positive association between *Keju* and achieving the position of chief minister, mediated by becoming a provincial military commissioner or Hanlin academian, lends credence to the notion that the pathways from *Keju* to chief minister, via these roles, reflect the developments post-755 CE at a systematic scale.

Figure 4 reports results obtained by using **X** (which includes the *Keju* variable) and the fixed effects from the specification in Section 3.1 as the right-hand side for four models. In the total effect model, the outcome variable is a binary indicator for chief minister appointment. In the two mediator models, the

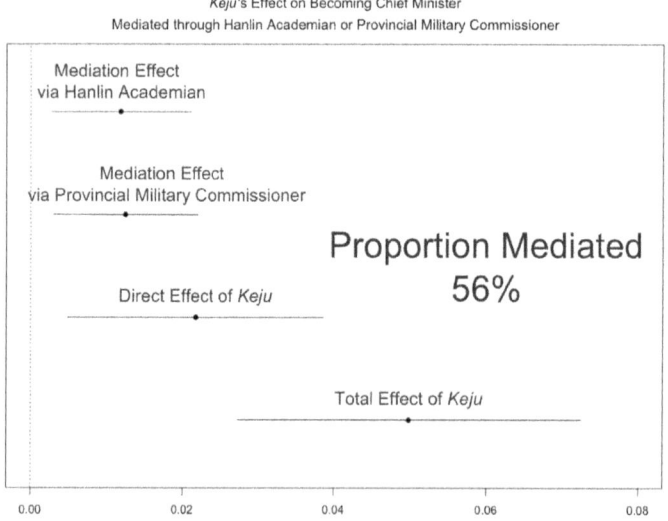

Figure 4 The direct and indirect effects of having passed the *Keju* on becoming a chief minister, with 95% confidence intervals

outcomes are binary indicators for Hanlin Academy appointment and provincial military commissioner appointment, respectively. In the direct effect model, we regress chief minister appointment on the right-hand side from the first three models plus the Hanlin Academy and commissioner appointments as two mediators. We run these analyses using data consisting of epitaphs examined in Wen, Wang, and Hout (2024), but we restrict the focus to individuals who died after 755 CE. We match this restricted dataset with our original dataset of Hanlin academians and data for provincial military commissioners from Chen and Wang (2024).

Our quantitative results show that *Keju* is a strong predictor of chief minister appointment, and as much as 56% of this effect is mediated by the stepping stones of Hanlin academian and provincial commissioner. These analyses suggest that, in the eyes of the elites, the lucrative pathways from *Keju* to chief minister had become clear in the latter half the Tang. They thus confirm our narrative that exogenous political and institutional developments further buttress the self-reinforcing nature of the *Keju* institution.

3.3 Conclusion

This section continues to highlight the gradual nature of *Keju*'s evolution, making its rising importance hard to discern initially. Since the late 7th century, however, both quantitative and qualitative analyses suggest that *Keju* had increasingly become the game in town for political selection regarding top government positions. *Keju*'s significance for overall social mobility had also dramatically risen over time, while the importance of aristocratic pedigree for officeholding rapidly diminished. The Tang emperors eventually recognized *Keju*'s role in expanding the "selectorate," and consequently took consistent efforts to preserve such equalizing potential. Other political and institutional developments facilitating the rise of provincial military commissioners and the Hanlin academians further enhanced and entrenched elites' incentives to compete in the *Keju*. Abundant evidence makes it clear that *Keju* in the Tang dynasty played a far more significant role than the "mere sideshow" characterization suggested by Kung (2022).

4 Evolution of *Keju* over Time

This section traces the development of *Keju* from the 10th century until its eventual demise in the early 20th century. Leveraging micro-level individual data from over 74,000 *Jinshi* degree holders (*Jinshi*, in the second millennium, refers to those who passed the *Keju* exams) across multiple dynasties, we unveil the implicit selection criteria embedded within the *Keju* system. In addition, complemented by information on more than 2,100 top government officials (ministers) and their descendants from various dynasties, we investigate the correlation between exam performance and career outcomes. The goal is to shed light not only on the selection criteria of *Keju* per se but also on general political selection in the imperial government.

Our findings reveal a diminishing impact of family background on the career trajectories of elite descendants. Two changes have occurred over the centuries after the Tang dynasty. First, *Keju* became increasingly competitive, and the influence of family background on exam performance declined substantially.[74] Second and especially since the 14th century, non-*Keju* pathways to offices in the civilian government were gradually shut down, and *Keju* became the vital element in shaping one's political career. The combined outcome was that, over the millennium after the Tang dynasty, the top political elites found it increasingly difficult to pass power onto their children. And political participation was extended to a larger portion of the population. These insights suggest a pivotal role played by the *Keju* system in mitigating the perpetuation of political power within elite familial circles. This section and the next will report the empirical results and discuss them in conjunction with political economy theories.

A clarification on the terms "aristocracy" and "elite" is necessary before proceeding. In medieval European contexts, "aristocracy" and "nobility" often refer to heritable titles bestowed by a monarch. While similar titles and enfeoffment certainly existed in imperial China, they by themselves did not signal profound political influence within the Chinese imperial bureaucracy beyond their legal privileges. The "medieval Chinese aristocracy," as studied in Sections 2 and 3, was not defined by such government-sanctioned titles. Instead, it was a sociopolitical status based on a family's perceived political influence, economic power, and cultural capital. A historian of medieval China has compared the medieval Chinese aristocracy, especially during the Tang dynasty, not to the knights and dukes of medieval Europe but to the senatorial aristocracy of the Roman empire (Tackett, 2014).

In contrast, the term "elite," as used in Sections 2 and 3, refers to a broader group that included the aristocracy but also encompassed other privileged individuals. This group was viewed as a higher stratum above commoners and merchants, with the aristocracy being the most socially prominent within it.

---

[74] Section 3 already identifies a negligible influence of family background on exam success among the Tang elites. It's important to note, however, that the Tang elites constituted a relatively select group. Within this group, some were descendants of aristocratic families, while others hailed from less prestigious but still affluent landowning families. Predominantly, these elites resided in or near the capitals. From the 10th century onward, the composition of elites broadened, becoming more diverse and localized.

This section and Section 5 focus on the second millennium after the Tang dynasty. Since the medieval Chinese aristocracy had largely disappeared by the 10th century, we will no longer use the term "aristocracy." Instead, we will use "elite" in a broader and looser sense, consistent with how the term is commonly used in political science literature, except in cases where formal models define it specifically. In our empirical analyses, particularly those underpinning Figures 10–12, we do define "top political elites" concretely as ministers and their sons.

4.1 *Keju*'s Development After the Tang

Peasant uprisings and the ensuing warlordism since 880 CE was an exogenous shock that further shaped the *Keju* system. Research within the "Tang-Song Transition" tradition argues that these violent upheavals, which particularly devastated the Tang capitals, effectively eliminated the medieval Chinese aristocracy (Tackett, 2014, 2020). As shown in Section 3 and Wen, Wang, and Hout (2024), however, the aristocracy's advantage in officeholding had already declined significantly before 880 CE.

This shock was nevertheless significant because it dramatically altered the *political geography* of ruler–elite relations. During the Tang, most top political elites, aristocratic or otherwise, were concentrated in the capitals, Chang'an and Luoyang, which were themselves geographically close and connected. This high concentration made it unsurprising that regional quota for *Keju* – which would limit the number of candidates from each province, including the capitals – were never strictly enforced during the Tang. With the centralized elites effectively eliminated, the new rulers, such as those of the Song dynasty (960–1279 CE), were able to implement a quota system that ensured more balanced representation across regions compared to the capital-heavy Tang period, a principle that later dynasties all followed rigorously.

The Song rulers also implemented several other changes. Under the Song system, regular exams were held every three years, progressing from the prefectural level to the central government and then the imperial court. Stringent measures were implemented to prevent cheating or favoritism. Exam papers were transcribed and anonymized. Notably, candidates were strictly forbidden from circulating their essays and poems in the capital before the exams to prevent influencing the examiners with their writings (Chen, 2017). To encourage widespread participation, the imperial government funded a network of public schools at the prefecture level across the nation.

The reforms implemented during this era not only established *Keju* as a cornerstone of governance but also encouraged broader societal participation in the political sphere. Significantly, advancements in paper-making and printing technologies contributed to this period of social transformation. Although paper had long existed in China, its production became substantially more cost-effective and accessible in early Song. This resulted in an unprecedented surge in book production throughout the Song, making education feasible and attainable for a larger population (Ho, 1962; Cheng, Stasavage, and Wang, 2023).

The Mongol invasion in the 13th century briefly interrupted *Keju*. However, it didn't take long for the Mongol-Yuan administration to acknowledge the merits of *Keju*. In 1315, they reinstated *Keju*, heavily borrowing from the structures and curriculum of the Song era. Nonetheless, political access remained largely restricted. After all, the Yuan dynasty was established by an alien ethnic minority, and the highest echelons of power remained reserved for nobles of this minority.

Following this temporary setback, *Keju* entered a second phase of rapid development with the ascension of the Ming dynasty (1368–1644 CE). *Keju* exams since the Ming followed a three-level structure similar to that of the Song. To become eligible for the first level of *Keju* exam, one had to pass other qualification exams. During this period, public schools gained increased prominence, extending their reach from prefectural to county levels. Several imperial decrees directly from the emperors mandated the establishment of public schools in every county throughout the country. Quotas were rigorously enforced to maintain relatively balanced representation from different regions of the country and prevent dominance by any single area. Over the Ming dynasty's 277-year reign, a total of eighty-nine regular exams took place, averaging around eighty-nine *Jinshi* degree holders (those who passed the exam) annually. This resulted in a considerable number of *Jinshi* degree holders, totaling more than 24,000. Although *Keju* encountered a brief disruption during the Manchu invasion in the 17th century, it quickly resumed regular operations and retained its central role in bureaucratic recruitment.

Keju finally met its end in 1905. The Manchu-Qing dynasty (1644–1911 CE) government grappled with significant external pressures from colonial powers and internal demands for modernization reforms. As a symbol of entrenched traditions and perceived backwardness, the rulers of the declining dynasty eventually abolished the 1,300-year-old institution.

To quantitatively demonstrate the evolution of the *Keju*, in Figure 5, we plot the annual number of *Jinshi* (进士) degree holders (Jinshi, hereafter). The *Jinshi* were individuals who passed the highest level of exams and were legitimate for government positions. The annual number of *Jinshi* can serve as a proxy for the scale of the *Keju*. A fifty-year moving average is taken to smooth out excessive fluctuations in the time series. The time trend in Figure 5 matches

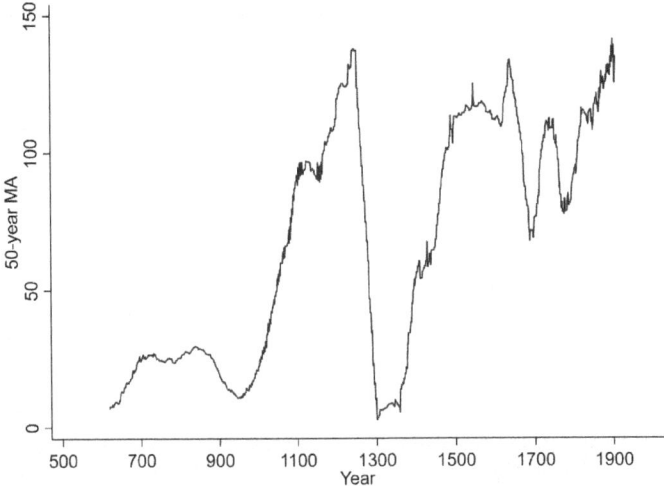

Figure 5 Average number of Jinshi degree holders per year

the historical narratives mentioned above, with two boosts recorded during the Song and the Ming dynasties and two busts during the Yuan (13th century) and the early Qing dynasties (17th century). Overall, it has been a relatively consistent institution throughout the millennium, enabling our cross-time analysis in this section.

In what follows, we quantitatively trace the development of the *Keju* across time through four dynasties from the 10th century till 1903. By leveraging biographic information and exam ranking of approximately 74,000 *Jinshi* degree holders from various time periods, we aim to uncover the selection criteria of the *Keju*. As a complement, we also compile a dataset of more than 2,100 ministers from the 2nd-century BCE until the end of imperial China to illustrate changes in the composition of the ruling elites. The main takeaway is that *Keju* limited political reproduction within the top elite families.

The data comes from multiple sources. Data on *Jinshi* degree holders comes from the Chinese Biographic Database (CBDB), which includes the name, exam year, birth year, family relationships, hometowns, and other basic biographic information of more than 74,000 candidates. We complement this data with other sources. We hand-collected information on the ranking of the Song dynasty *Jinshi* degree holders based on *Song-dai Deng-ke Zong-lu* (2014), while that of the Ming dynasty is from Huang and Yang (2022). The ranking of the Qing dynasty *Jinshi* is based on original records in the CBDB. Family relations and their government positions for the Song and the Ming dynasties come from the CBDB and Huang and Yang (2022), respectively. Population data is digitized based on the *Historical Atlas of China* (2012) and is available for the years 1102, 1290, 1391, 1460, 1565, and 1820. We also collect information on government ministers for the entire imperial period based on the official *Twenty-Four Histories* of the Chinese dynasties, which is then matched with the CBDB to retrieve additional family information. The following subsections discuss the variables and regression models. More details on data and variable construction can be found in the Online Appendix.

4.2 The Selection Criteria of *Keju*

In this subsection, we use a regression model to uncover the implicit selection criteria of the *Keju* and trace their development over time. With quantitative analysis, we hope to answer a few simple questions: What factors contributed to a candidate's success in *Keju*? And how did the relative importance of different factors change over time?

Specifically, the major outcome variable we examined is a dummy variable, which equals one if the candidate ranked among the top three during his cohort (i.e. *Tier One*, 一甲) and zero otherwise. Here, we use a dummy for the top-tier candidates instead of the general ranking for all candidates largely because of data availability.[75] Since this subsection focuses on capturing the time trends rather than quantifying the coefficients, we use the top-tier dummy as our primary outcome variable. In the Online Appendix, we also use the general ranking and the regional total number of *Jinshi* as robustness checks, and the findings are similar. Because all the data points are *Jinshi* themselves, our analyses using "top tier" as the outcome among the *Jinshi*s are comparisons *within* those who passed the *Keju* exam. These intensive margin analyses are nonetheless important because a "top tier" was a prominent status in and of itself and those who earned the honor were more likely to enter the bureaucracy via higher-ranked or more prestigious offices than those taken by their peers in the same *Jinshi* cohort.

The two main independent variables we examine are: (a) family background, indicated by whether a candidate's father held government positions before him, and (b) regional economic development, indicated by the population density of the candidate's hometown.[76] Readers may notice that the characterization of family background here differs from that in Section 3. In Section 3, we decompose "medieval aristocracy" into two dimensions. The first one is

---

[75] The data on the general ranking of all *Jinshi* is only available for the Ming and the Qing dynasties, while data on the top tier *Jinshi* is available from the 10th century till the end of the imperial period.

[76] Population density is calculated at the one-degree grid cell level (number of individuals per squared kilometer). We standardize the variable based on the standard deviation of nationwide population distribution in that year to control for overall population growth.

based on the power of the immediate ancestors, measured by the ranks of the highest offices held by one's father and grandfather. The second one hinges on the pedigree of the bloodline itself, proxied with membership in a prominent aristocratic branch. Throughout this section, we omit the second dimension of ancestral prominence and revert back to a one-dimensional measurement based on the father's officeholding.

There are two reasons for this approach. First of all, the second dimension had already ceased to matter in political selection even during the Tang dynasty, when the so-called medieval aristocracy was still in existence (Section 3.1; e.g. Wu, 1992; Lu, 2016; Wen, Wang, and Hout, 2024). With the utter disappearance of the aristocracy in post-Song times, historians almost unanimously agree that bloodline pedigree never regained its prominence.[77] Father's officeholding would be a more appropriate proxy to measure politically privileged family background for this sample period. Secondly and more importantly, this section aims to document the temporal evolution of the *Keju*. To this end, father's officeholding is a measure that can be easily applied to different time periods and retains a relatively consistent and straightforward interpretation. Hence, we use father's officeholding as our main measurement of family background.

We employ several model specifications. The benchmark model includes only two variables, *Father Office* and *Population Density*, plus a time fixed effect. The regression equation is as follows:

$$logit(\text{RankTopTier}_{ijt}) = \beta_0 + \beta_1 Father_{ijt} + \beta_2 PopDensity_{jt} + \alpha_t + \epsilon_{ijt}. \quad (1)$$

In this preferred model, we intentionally do not control for province fixed effects. There were ample examples of prominent political families throughout Chinese history who derived power from regional affiliations. Political reproduction within elite families could thus be intertwined with or disguised as regional inequalities in political access. Since this subsection focuses on capturing the overall family impact on *Keju* success, we want to include the part of the effect disguised as regional inequality as well.

In the revised models, we include province fixed effects, as well as individual controls, such as age, household registration status (such as civilian, military, artisan, or merchant), parental status (alive or deceased), and exam fields (such as poetry, rites, and classic books). Table 1 summarizes the regression results. The estimation of the preferred model is given in Column (1), while Columns (2)–(4) provide various robustness checks.

---

[77] Membership in local clans (宗族) during the second millennium carried much less weight in terms of signaling an individual's distinct political status as a quantitative measure.

Table 1 Selection criteria of the *Keju*, whole sample

Variables	(1) Dummy_top3	(2) Dummy_top3	(3) Rank_inv	(4) Rank_inv	(5) Rank_inv
Dummy_ father office	0.735***	1.139***	0.0927***	11.33***	0.0768***
	(0.187)	(0.403)	(0.0195)	(1.696)	(0.0245)
Pop density	0.315***	0.539***	0.0481***	5.113***	0.0314*
	(0.0830)	(0.144)	(0.0126)	(1.799)	(0.0169)
Age	0.00513	0.0964	−0.0099***	−1.113***	−0.0116***
	(0.0168)	(0.0849)	(0.00159)	(0.154)	(0.00239)
Urban center	−0.0162	−0.305*	−0.0111*	−0.527	−0.0151**
	(0.0527)	(0.165)	(0.00598)	(0.985)	(0.00724)
Household status		Y			Y
Parental status		Y			Y
Exam field		Y			Y
Model	Logit	Logit	Rank order logit	Panel	Rank order logit
FE	Year	Year	Prov	Prov-Year	Prov
Observations	12,511	3,962	12,463	12,457	8,051

Note: The unit of analysis is individual. Robust standard errors are in parentheses. *** indicates $p < 0.01$, ** $p < 0.05$, and * $p < 0.1$.

Overall, both family political background and regional economic development contributed positively to exam success. The coefficients are positive and consistent throughout different model specifications. In terms of the magnitude of the impact, based on the preferred model in Column (1), having a father who was a government official would, on average, increase a candidate's odds of obtaining the top tier ranks by 108%. Similarly, when the candidate's hometown population density increased by one unit of national standard deviation, his odds of obtaining the top tier ranks would increase by 37%.[78] To interpret the magnitude in terms of probability, the average probability of obtaining the top tier ranks is 2.14% for candidates with father officials and 1.38% for others, which is equal to a 55% increase for candidates with father officials.

In the following, we move on to another main task of this section – to uncover the evolution of *Keju* selection criteria over time. We still employ a logistic regression model similar to Equation (1). However, instead of estimating the average impact of a variable for the whole sample, we employ a flexible

---

[78] The odds are different from the probabilities. Let p denote the probability of passing the exam. Then, the odds of passing the exam would be $p/(1-p)$.

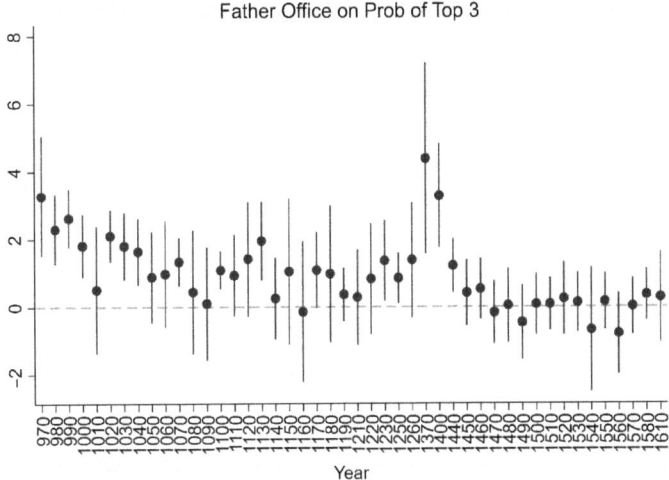

Figure 6 The impact of family background on exam ranking

Note: the coefficients plotted in Figure 6 to 8 are logit coefficients, not the marginal impact on top-tier probability.

estimating equation that evaluates the impact of the variables separately for every decade.

We first examine family background in isolation. Figure 6 plots the impact of *Father Office* on exam ranking with no controls other than year fixed effects. From the beginning of the Song dynasty around 970 CE until the end of the Ming in the early 17th century, the impact of *Father Office* has been largely positive but with a declining magnitude. The only exception to this pattern was the early Ming dynasty when the newly established imperial government periodically reverted to recruitment based on recommendation (Hucker, 2008). This exception was quickly corrected, however, within a few decades.

We then examine the impact of regional economic development. Figure 7 plots a similar graph for *Population Density* with no controls other than year fixed effects. The coefficients for *Population Density* show a consistent and increasing trend throughout the millennium. The impact rose from mild significance in the early 11th century to significantly positive toward the end of the imperial period, with growing magnitudes.

Figure 8 performs a multivariate logistic regression, including both *Father Office* and *Population Density* as independent variables. Because there is a substantial gap in the coverage of the two variables, the coefficients of this multivariate regression are estimated for every fifty years. The pattern remains the same. The impact of family background weakened over time, whereas that of regional economic development strengthened. In other words, the exam

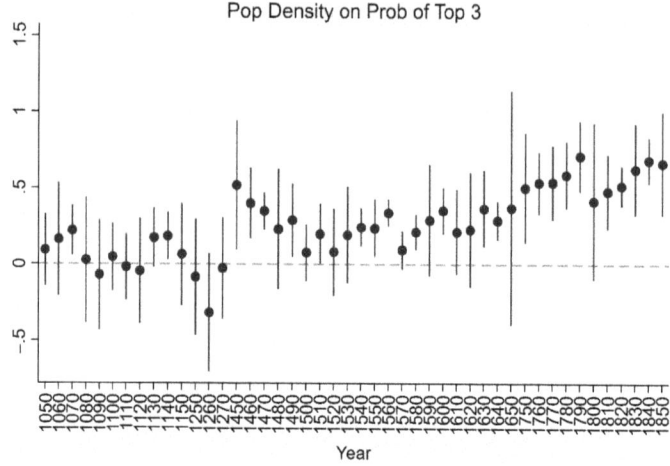

Figure 7 The impact of regional economic development on exam ranking

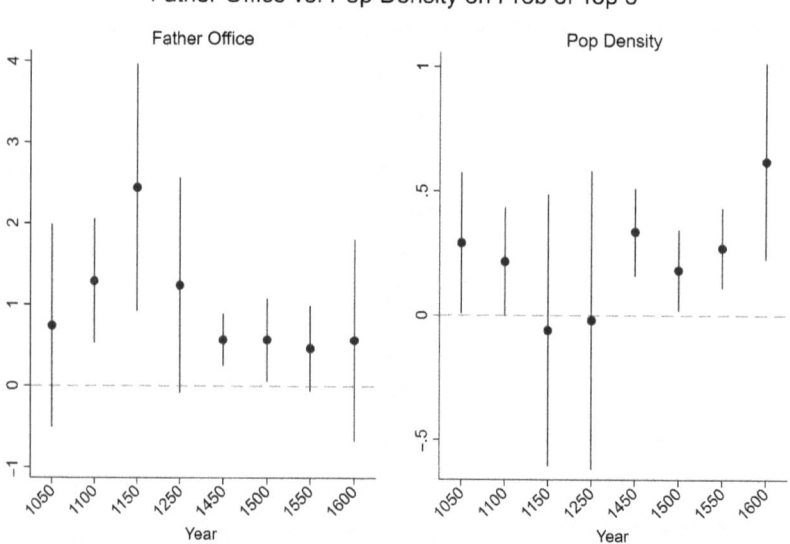

Figure 8 Multivariate regression, family background vs. regional development

ranking increasingly reflected the regional economic development level rather than the political connection of the candidate's family.

The evidence fits well with the prevailing narrative in the literature. Historians largely agreed on the increasingly competitive nature of the *Keju* in the late imperial period. Several historians, such as Ho (1962), Chaffee (1995), and

Elman (2013), noted that consecutive governments during this period initiated a number of reforms to make the *Keju* more impartial and equitable and, by extension, more competitive. The exams of the Tang emphasized poetry and prose, which allowed a certain level of flexibility to demonstrate creativity and individuality but also more room for subjective interpretation. The retention of poetry and prose in the exams became a focal point of debate and reform during the Song (Chaffee, 1995, p. 71), and was abruptly ended at the beginning of the Ming (Elman, 2013). A new school of interpretation for the Confucian canons, sometimes called *Neo-Confucianism*, became the political orthodoxy for the *Keju* since the 14th century onward. During the Ming dynasty, *Keju* experienced further narrowing of its content with the eight-legged essay legislated as the only permitted format (Elman, 2013). Over time, the exam increasingly emphasized memorization and moral cultivation, especially concerning loyalty to the emperor, and allowed less room for improvisation. The intellectual merit of these reforms is highly debatable, but they could help level the playing field for the less privileged or less connected.

Additional procedures were also introduced to minimize clientelism. During the Tang dynasty, it was not only permissible but also desirable for candidates to submit samples of their writing to examiners before the date of the exam, so that "reputation and character" could be taken into account. This practice was discontinued during the Song, when strict anonymization protocols were introduced during the Song dynasty (Chaffee, 1995). Not only were the names of the candidates covered, but the exam papers were also transcribed before being presented to the examiners to ensure that the handwriting would not betray the identity of the candidates.[79] These protocols were followed by later dynasties. Bribing and cheating in the *Keju* exams were considered a felony and punishable by demotion, flogging, exile, and even death.

As a demonstration of the impact of these reforms, the number of individuals participating in the exams grew substantially, and *Keju* became much more competitive. Chaffee (1995, p. 35) noted that, despite a relatively stable quota of successful candidates passing the first stage prefectural exams (*Ju-ren*s, 举人), the average ratio of successful candidates to the number of participants decreased from 5/10 in the year 1009 to 1/200 in 1275. Assembling information from various sources and local gazetteers, Chaffee's (1995) estimation illustrates a remarkable growth of participants in the first-stage exams

---

[79] The practice of covering candidates' names was initiated for the palace exam in 992 and extended to the metropolitan exams in 1007 and the provincial exams in 1033. The practice of transcribing exam papers was initiated for the palace and metropolitan exams in 1015 and extended to provincial exams in 1037 (Chaffee, 1995, p. 51).

not just in absolute numbers but also as a percentage of the total population.[80] For the Ming–Qing period, according to estimates by Elman (2013, p. 152), there were some 30,000 licentiates (i.e. individuals allowed to participate in the first-stage provincial exams) out of an approximate population of 85 million around the year 1400, a ratio of almost one licentiate per 2,800 persons. In 1700, this increased to 500,000 licentiates in a total population of 268 million, or a ratio of one licentiate per 540 persons.[81]

There are at least three points that we can take away from these numbers. First, the number of exam participants had grown substantially in the late imperial period, and this must have made the exams more competitive. Second, even though *Keju* was probably never truly accessible for the entire male population because of financial reasons, the percentage that had indeed participated in the exams was still very impressive. It would not be much of a stretch to conclude that *Keju* in the late imperial period broadened political participation to the lower elites or even some commoners. Lastly, from an alternative perspective, the cost of exam preparation was substantial. The fact that more and more people from humbler backgrounds found it worthwhile to give it a try suggests that the perceived advantage of family background in *Keju* must have declined remarkably, as can be seen in Figures 6–8.

4.3 Political Reproduction within the Elites

The preceding subsection examines the selection criteria employed within the *Keju* system. However, for many readers, the broader interest lies not in *Keju* per se but, rather, in the criteria shaping overall political selection. This subsection directs attention toward the interaction between *Keju* and political selection in general. Here, we focus on the apex of the political hierarchy – the central government's top officials. The driving inquiries underpinning this subsection are simple: Who constituted the upper echelons of governmental authority? Did ascension to these positions necessitate familial affiliations or exceptional performance in the *Keju*? Moreover, how did the relative significance of diverse determinants evolve over time?

---

[80] Chaffee (1995, p. 38) provided several estimated time series of the percentage of adult males taking the prefectural exam for different parts of the country. Most of the series increased from below 0.5% in the 11th century to above 2% in the 13th century. These ratios are much higher than those in the later Ming–Qing period, partly due to the smaller population of the Song dynasty and partly the fact that the Southern Song covered mostly the southern parts of China, which had stronger literary traditions.

[81] Beginning in the 15th century, each stage of the *Keju* selection process eliminated a vast majority of candidates. According to Elman's (2013) estimation, the odds for success in all stages of the selection process were perhaps only slightly better than one in 6,000 (or 0.01%) during the Qing.

To answer these questions, we gathered information on a list of top government officials from the beginning of the imperial period in the 2nd-century BCE till the early 20th century. They were the "chief operating officers" or "ministers" of the central dynastic governments. The criteria for inclusion in this dataset require holding the highest official positions, directly answering to the emperor, and managing the daily operation of the government. Among these figures are prominent examples such as the Three Excellencies (*San-gong*, 三公) from the Qin–Han dynasty, the Grand Secretariats (*Da-xue-shi*, 大学士) during the Ming–Qing period, the Grand Councillor (*Jun-ji-da-chen*, 军机大臣) of the Qing dynasty, and those colloquially referred to as "chief minister" (宰相) in the Tang and Song. A comprehensive list of positions included in the dataset can be found in the Online Appendix. To streamline discussions, we will henceforth refer to these top government officials as "ministers."

The data covers the major dynasties as well as the short-lived ones that are sometimes overlooked, such as the Liao, the Jin, and the Five Dynasties. This effort yields a dataset of 2,441 ministers, with records of names, positions, years in office, and modes for entering office, such as inheritance (*men-yin*, 门荫), imperial service exam (*Keju*), or military exam (*Wu-ju*, 武举). We then manually match the ministers after the 7th century (post-Tang era) with our *Jinshi* to retrieve their exam performance, if any, and with the CBDB dataset to obtain their biographic information and kinship networks. The CBDB offers comprehensive coverage of biographic information of historical individuals in China, including kinship relationships and government positions, which we utilize to identify the family backgrounds of the ministers.[82] For more information on the minister dataset, please see the Online Appendix.

Figure 9 plots the percentage of ministers with examination backgrounds, including informal or irregular exams preceding the formal *Keju* institution. Panel (a) uses a 50-year moving average, while (b) uses a 100-year moving average. There is a substantial upward trend in the percentage of ministers coming from exam backgrounds – the ratio started from zero before the 6th century and soared to above 80% in the Ming dynasty. The ratio dipped at the beginning of each dynasty when new political hierarchies were established, likely based on military successes. Yet, the temporary setbacks did not derail the overall upward trend.

---

[82] The data on government officials in the CBDB includes both positions in the administrative branches, such as positions in the ministries, positions in the military, such as army generals, and enfeoffment positions that were passed on by inheritance. Hence, it is a relatively comprehensive measure of political power and elite status. In this analysis, we include any kind of government title as a government position.

56 *Political Economy*

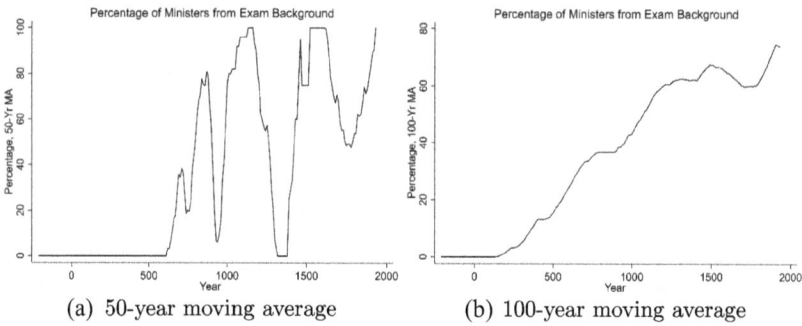

Figure 9 Percentage of ministers with examination background

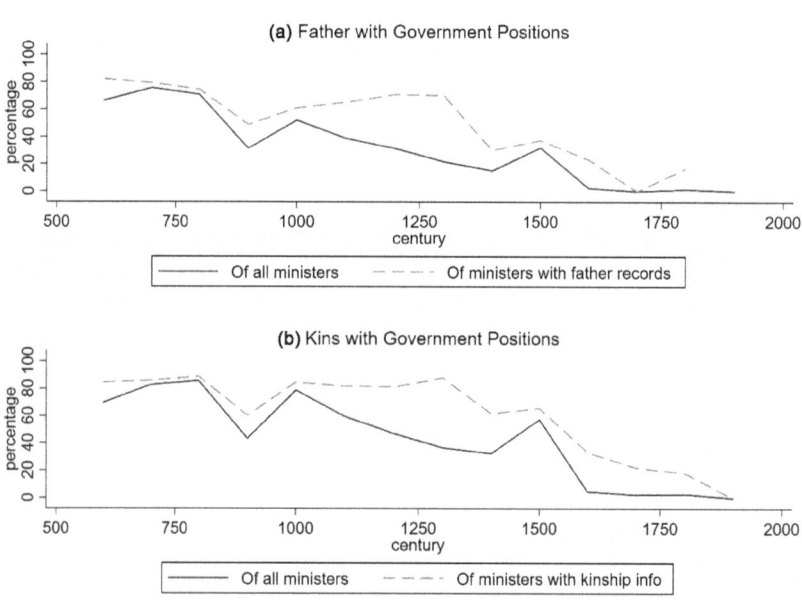

Figure 10 Family background of ministers

What about the family backgrounds of the ministers? In Figure 10(a), we present the century-average percentage of ministers whose fathers held government positions previously. The solid line traces the percentage of all ministers. As a robustness check to ensure data consistency across various dynasties, the dashed line is calculated as the percentage of ministers for whom father-related information is available. Notably, the index commenced at a remarkably high level when the Tang dynasty had just begun. Approximately 60%–80% of ministers in the 7th century had parental ties to the government, with several cases of father–son ministerial pairs.[83] However, this trend began to wane

---

[83] For notable examples of father–son ministers, please see the Online Appendix.

progressively over subsequent centuries, reaching an eventual low level of below 20% during the Qing dynasty.

One might raise the concern that parental officeholding was one of many channels through which family connections could play a role.[84] Marriage networks, as well as extended family connections, could also prove tremendously beneficial in historical China.[85] As a robustness check, Figure 10(b) plots a similar time trend for the percentage of ministers with at least one extended family member holding a government position within three older generations. Again, the solid line traces the percentage of all ministers, while the dashed line is calculated as a ratio of ministers with kinship information available.[86] The pattern remains similar. Both Figure 10(a) and (b) confirm a downward trend in ministers' elite family backgrounds after the Tang dynasty and more significantly after the Song.[87]

Now we have some evidence to answer the question raised at the beginning of the subsection: Who became the top officials in imperial China? The answer

---

[84] Two objections are frequently raised against using paternal officeholding as an indicator of family political background. One is the high mortality rate in premodern times. And the second objection concerns the important role that extended family relations played in historical China. The combination of the two factors suggests that political elites might choose to pass power and privilege not to their direct male descendants but to their extended family members (Hartwell, 1982; Hymes, 1986). Even though we fully acknowledge this phenomenon, we believe that paternal officeholding is a meaningful indicator in our setting because our analysis focuses on cross-time comparison. There is no apparent reason to believe that the mortality rate or the importance of extended family relations was more significant in the late imperial periods than in the early times. Moreover, it fits human nature that, if one had a choice, he would prefer to benefit his direct offspring rather than members of the extended family. The fact that the political elite had to maintain the family status through an extended family network implies the existence of some external constraints.

[85] For example, Shiue (2016) shows that conditional on the father, grandfathers play only a minor role in the social status of the son, but nonlinear relationships to uncles and the extended family of in-laws matters.

[86] For this revised indicator, officeholdings of any relatives (both maternal and paternal) of the same or within three older generations (not the descendants) are counted.

[87] One might worry that differences in record-keeping across dynasties could be driving the observed pattern. If ministers from elite families were consistently recorded while those from commoner backgrounds were only occasionally, dynasties with less comprehensive record-keeping would stand out as having a higher percentage of ministers from elite families. We address this concern by comparing two indicators: (a) ministers from families with officeholding traditions as a percentage of all ministers, and (b) ministers from families with officeholding traditions as a percentage of ministers with family information available. If the recorded samples were representative of all ministers, then indicator (b) would illustrate the average family background of ministers. On the other hand, if only ministers from elite families were recorded consistently over time, then (a) would be a better indicator. If reality was somewhere between the two scenarios, meaning that recorded samples were biased toward ministers from elite families but not consistently, then (a) would be a lower bound estimate. We examine both indicators in Figure 10; the trends are similar. The result confirms that the pattern shown in Figure 10 is not due to inconsistent record-keeping.

is that since the late Tang and especially since the Song dynasty, an increasingly larger portion of ministers had exam backgrounds and came from less politically prominent families.

The evidence presented here shows the increasing *popularity* of Keju among the political elites. Unfortunately, it cannot be used as direct evidence to prove the *importance* of *Keju* in determining one's political career. One potential confounding factor is the growing population of exam candidates. Even if *Keju* had no impact on the political career of officials, we would still see a larger percentage of ministers with exam backgrounds simply because the underlying population with *Jinshi* degrees had grown larger. This is an inherent issue with studies that suffer from *survival bias* – a problem that happens when one focuses on the successful few and ignores the ones who did not make it.

To address the survival bias, we need a sample that includes both those who made it and those who did not. We construct such a sample by collecting information on the ministers' sons.[88] The ministers serve as a sample of the top political elites, excluding the royal families. The career outcomes of their sons can be an indicator to illustrate the level of political reproduction within the top elite families.

Figure 11 examines the career outcomes of the ministers' sons over time. In Panel (a), the solid line shows the century-average percentage of ministers with at least one son obtaining a government position. This indicator is calculated as a percentage of all ministers, while the dashed line provides a robustness check, using the subsample of ministers with son records as the denominator.[89] Panel (a) shows that the percentage of ministers' sons who obtained government positions had declined substantially since the latter half of the Tang dynasty – a pattern that perfectly echoes Figure 10. Furthermore, this declining trend became even sharper later on. If we treat the year 1200 as the dividing year, around 49% of ministers could secure government positions for at least one of their sons before the 13th century. That ratio dropped remarkably afterward and eventually reached an average of 5.6% after the 16th century.

Admittedly, this index can be subject to several limitations. Most notably, the records of government officials may not be consistent over time. To address this

---

[88] Here, we only examine one generation down. The reason is that the more generations we cover, the more likely we will end up with a sample that favors successful families. At the ministerial level, it is reasonable that most of their sons would have records regardless of their personal achievements.

[89] For the solid line indicator, a minister with missing data is treated as not having a son obtaining either achievement. We provide more discussion and additional robustness checks on this point in the Online Appendix.

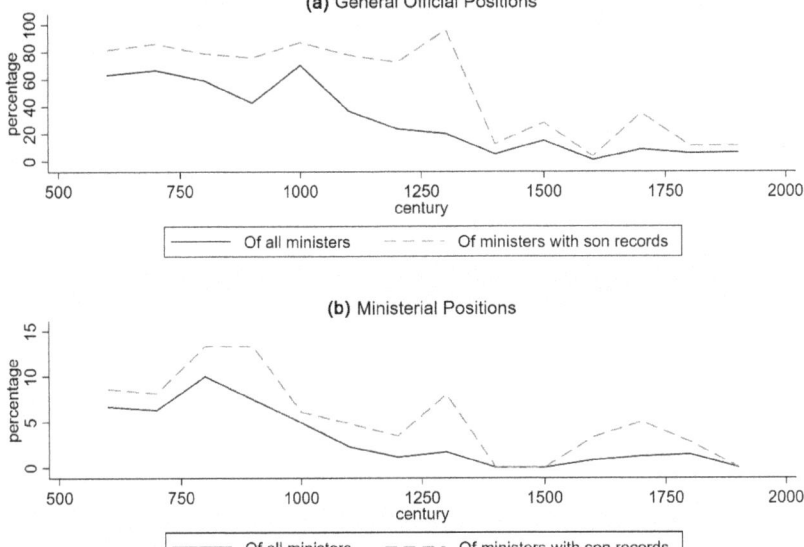

Figure 11 Career outcome for ministers' sons

issue, we recalculated a similar index based on the portion of ministers' sons who obtained top ministerial positions. The justification for this approach is that we have much more complete records of ministers, compared to data on general official positions. Hence, we can safely treat a missing data point as a negative value for ministerial positions. Figure 11(b) plots this modified index, and the pattern remains similar. In the Online Appendix, we perform more robustness checks on the career outcomes of ministers' offspring, including their grandchildren, and the pattern remains the same.

Both Figures 10 and 11 confirm the same phenomenon – that the level of power perpetuation within the top elite families, at least at the minister level, had started to decline since the Tang dynasty and more dramatically since the 11th century.[90]

To shed light on the cause of this decline, we examine the impact of a *Jinshi* degree (passing the *Keju* exam) on the career outcome of a minister's son using the following regression model:

$$Office_{it} = \Sigma_s \beta_s Jinshi_{it} \cdot Dummy_{st} + \alpha_t + \epsilon_{it}, \qquad (2)$$

---

[90] One concern is that the records of officeholding may not be consistent over time. As of May 2023, the CBDB has 3,082 records of officeholding for the Tang dynasty, 10,899 for the Song, 3,539 for the Yuan, 58,340 for the Ming, and 19,222 for the Qing. Data coverage for the Ming–Qing period is at least comparable to earlier times, if not better. The declining trend observed in Figure 11 is not likely due to data coverage issues.

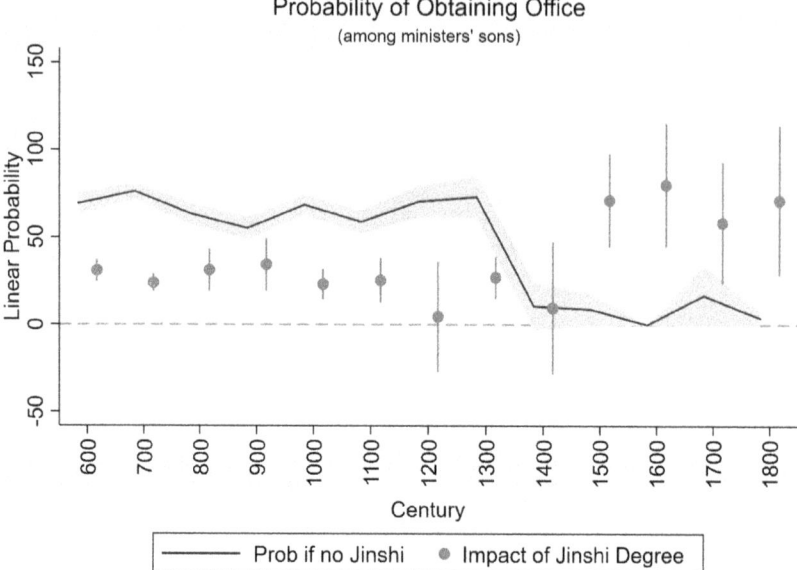

Figure 12 Regression on career outcomes for ministers' sons, subsample

where i index the individual and t the century. The century $Dummy_{st}$ equals one when s equals t, and zero otherwise. This equation estimates a series of century-specific *Jinshi* impacts β_s. The goal of the equation is to trace the fluctuations in the impact of *Jinshi* degrees across different time periods.

The results are plotted in Figure 12. For comparison, the solid trend line plots the average probability of obtaining an office for a minister's son if he had no *Jinshi* degree. The vertical confidence intervals are the estimated additional impacts of a *Jinshi* degree. Figure 12 shows that the significance of having a *Jinshi* degree increased dramatically during the Ming–Qing period, at a time when the probability of securing a government position dropped for those without a degree.[91] Even though having a *Jinshi* degree had always been a positive factor, the magnitude of its impact rose substantially after the 15th century. Before the 14th century, having a *Jinshi* degree enhanced the probability of obtaining an office by 24 percentage points on average. Afterward, the average contribution of a *Jinshi* degree soared to a 58 percentage point increase in the probability. These statistics are based on the subsample of ministers with sons' information available, and, hence, not likely due to differences in data coverage.

---

[91] Here, we use a linear probability model rather than a logit because of its more straightforward interpretation. The result of a logit model is given in the Online Appendix, and the conclusions are similar.

Figure 12 illustrates a turning point in political selection during the 15th century. Two changes occurred simultaneously. First, success in the *Keju* became a more prominent predictor of career success. And secondly, it became much more challenging for the political elites to pass power onto their children outside the *Keju* system.

The evidence accords well with historians' observations. During the Song dynasty, hereditary privilege (*yin*, or royal protection, *men-yin* 门荫) was still an important way to enter office. Royal protection was a political privilege granted to relations of the royal family, top officials, or individuals with outstanding contributions to the empire. It allowed their descendants, usually their sons, to obtain some kind of office on the basis of birth. According to Chaffee (1995, p.25), in the year 1213, about 40.8% of administrative government officials in ranks six to nine held a *Jinshi* degree, while 52.5% entered offices through royal protection. During the Ming dynasty, until 1467, all civil officials of ranks one through seven, after certain years of satisfactory service, were entitled to "protect" (*yin*) one son or grandson each, who would become automatically eligible either for office or for enrollment as an imperial academy student. From 1467 on, this privilege was restricted to the highest-ranking officials, who were in ranks one through three, and those with enfeoffment. And even their heirs had to pass qualifying tests and could only be enrolled in the imperial academy, not directly appointed to office (Hucker, 2008). At the same time, the path of recommendation to officialdom almost disappeared by the late 15th century (Hucker, 2008, p. 30). By the Qing dynasty, the scope of the *yin* privilege was further restricted for civilian officials. Note that even prior to these efforts to curtail the *yin* privilege, it was already widely acknowledged among elite circles since the 9th century that those who entered the bureaucracy via royal protection generally would not be able to advance very far in the bureaucratic echelon. *Keju* had always been viewed as the most promising mode of entry since late Tang, and its perceived advantage over the *yin* only grew further with these aforementioned efforts to explicitly restrict the *yin* system.

By 1764, Ho (1962, p. 48) estimated that about 72.5% of local officials between seventh and fourth ranks, which formed the backbone of local administration, had a *Keju* background. In comparison, purchase contributed to 22.4% and *yin* privilege only 1%.[92] Similarly, relying on a completely different dataset of household registration in the 18th to the 19th century, Campbell and Lee (2003) show the existence of substantial downward mobility among the sons of prominent families, as well as upward mobility for the commoner, even after accounting for the influence of distant kin. The development of the *Keju* was

---

[92] For the purchase of offices in the Qing Dynasty, see the excellent research by Zhang (2022).

no doubt accompanied and, to some degree, aided by the gradual dismantling of elite privileges.

In summary, the results in this section illustrate a declining level of power perpetuation within the top elite families from the 10th to the 19th centuries. This phenomenon is likely driven by a combination of two forces. On the one hand, the *Keju* system itself became more competitive over time, and the advantage enjoyed by top elite families declined substantially. On the other hand, outside the *Keju* system, additional pathways to officeholding were gradually shut down or pushed away as secondary means. *Keju* was eventually elevated to a level that shadowed all other government recruitment methods in both scale and prestige. This long process also highlights that no institution at the scale of the *Keju* can be built overnight; it will require an extensive process and the co-development of supporting institutions.

4.4 Conclusion

To summarize, we provide two sets of quantitative evidence in this section. The first set of evidence illustrates the development of *Keju* and uncovers the implicit selection criteria it employed. The finding suggests that, since the 10th century (the earliest century for which data is available for this long-term analysis), exam performance reflected less on the family backgrounds of the candidates and more on regional economic development.

The second set of evidence investigates the overall rule of political selection in the imperial governments. We approximate the level of political reproduction among the top elite families using two measurements: the percentage of ministers with fathers or relatives holding government positions before them, and the percentage of ministers' sons who obtained government positions after them. Both indicators had started to decrease since the Tang dynasty and more rapidly after the Song, at a time when the *Keju* was further expanded and institutionalized. Using data on ministers' sons as a representative sample of the descendants of top elite families, we show that family background gradually lost weight in predicting an individual's political career. In comparison, exam performance remained a significant factor throughout the millennium and gained even more influence from the 14th century onward.

Combining results from both sides leads naturally to the conclusion that *Keju* had played a pivotal role in limiting the perpetuation of political power among elite families in historical China. At the very least, *Keju* helped maintain a selection rule that put limited weight on family backgrounds. All elites, except the royal family, were subject to political competition via *Keju*. The popularity and importance of *Keju* ensured that members of elite families would not be able to monopolize political access, and individuals from non-elite backgrounds could enter the political arena in a regular fashion. This would have helped reshuffle the political elite and prevent the emergence of powerful political families in competition with the royal family.

Lastly, the results in this section illustrate the gradual development of the *Keju* system and emphasize the coevolution of institutions. One of our main arguments is that *Keju* expanded political participation beyond the top elite families to include lower elites and even some wealthier commoners. However, *Keju* could not have achieved this on its own. Broader participation was made possible by the spread of books, the growth of schools, and dynastic support for educational infrastructure. Additionally, the rise of *Keju* was facilitated by the gradual dismantling of hereditary privileges outside the system. Just as Rome wasn't built in a day, an institution of *Keju*'s scale needed to be tested, contested, and refined over time.

5 *Keju* and Political Stability

This section investigates the intricate relationship between *Keju* and political stability. *Keju* was established in China during the 7th century. The idea of *Keju* later extended to other East Asian countries via traveling monks and diplomats. Analogous exam systems emerged in Korea (from 958 to 1894), Vietnam (from 1075 to 1913), Japan (briefly during the Heian period, 794–1185), and Ryukyu (from the early 15th century until the Japanese occupation in 1609). In Korea and Vietnam, *Keju* evolved into a pivotal – if not the preeminent – pathway to political offices, profoundly shaping their subsequent political and social development.

We first conduct a cross-country regression analysis encompassing 4,119 rulers across 112 historical states from the 1st to the 18th centuries. This empirical exercise reveals a positive relationship between the establishment of the *Keju* system and improvements in ruler stability. Remarkably, the magnitude of this correlation rivals the impact observed for the establishment of parliamentary systems in Europe.

Building upon the empirical evidence, we advance a theoretical discourse by synthesizing insights from various literatures to explore plausible mechanisms through which the *Keju* system may affect political stability. These mechanisms include the installation of meritocracy, expansion of the selectorate, augmentation of regional representation within the government, facilitation of social mobility, and the cultivation of a state ideology emphasizing homogeneity and loyalty toward the ruler.

5.1 Empirical Evidence on Stability

Western Europe witnessed a sustained increase in ruler duration since the 9th century (Blaydes and Chaney, 2013). Scholars emphasize the role of parliamentary institutions in facilitating political stability (e.g. Strayer, 1970, Downing, 1992). Parliaments offered powerholders a venue to communicate with each other, to bargain with the ruler collectively, and to exercise institutional checks and balances against the ruler. They thus facilitated the ruler's credible commitment to the preservation of the elite's interest, reducing incentives for coup or revolt (e.g. North and Weingast, 1989; Stasavage, 2003; Blaydes and Chaney, 2013).

Recall the prominent observation in Blaydes and Chaney (2013) that ruler duration in Europe outpaced that of the Muslim world since the 9th century. This divergence in political stability was rooted in Europe's "feudal revolution," which gave rise to executive constraints, culminating in the development of parliamentary institutions – an evolution not paralleled in the Middle East (Blaydes and Chaney, 2013). We now compare ruler duration in Europe with that of polities in East Asia, which, like the Middle East, lacked parliamentary institutions. However, unlike the Muslim world, all East Asian polities except Japan adopted the *Keju* system. Figure 13 compares the trends in ruler duration between Europe and East Asia from 800 CE, arguably the beginning year of Europe's "feudal revolution." We use data from Morby (1989) due to its broader temporal coverage compared to that of Blaydes and Chaney (2013). The dashed line substantively reproduces the observation in Blaydes and Chaney (2013) about the enhancement of ruler stability in Europe.

Interestingly, at various points in time, East Asia appeared to catch up with Europe in terms of ruler duration. The 100-year moving average of ruler duration in East Asia began increasing around the mid-9th century, with a sharp rise during the Northern Song dynasty, coinciding with the expansion of the *Keju* system and the implementation of additional institutions and policies that solidified its dominance. By the early 12th century, ruler duration in East Asia had even surpassed that of Europe. The trend dipped after northern China fell to several alien empires that would eventually be conquered by the Mongols, whose dynasty failed to regularize *Keju* except for a brief period. Also contributing to the dip were the various political upheavals during the Hojo regency in Japan's Kamakura period, a country that never adopted the *Keju*. However, following the Ming dynasty's founding in the 14th century, *Keju* was restored and further expanded (Section 4). Correspondingly, ruler duration in East Asia sharply increased once again, drawing much closer to European levels by the 19th century.

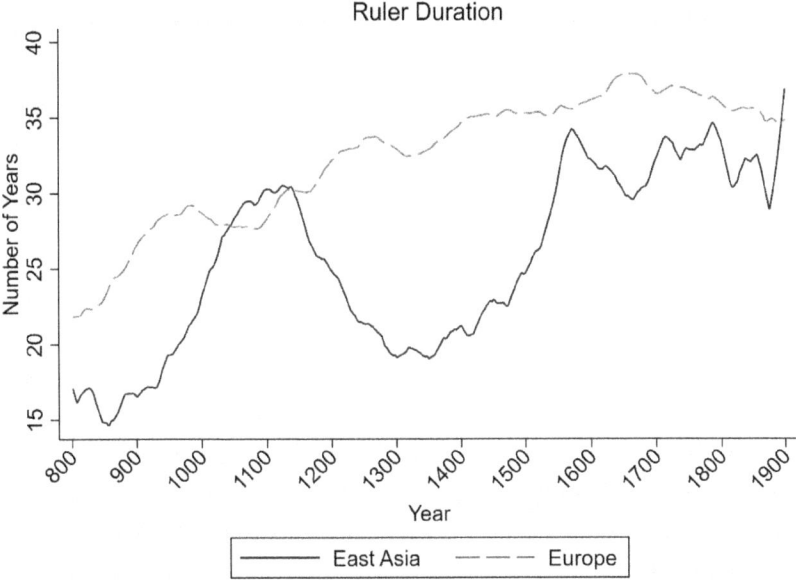

Figure 13 Ruler duration in East Asia and Europe

Note: The data is based on Morby (1989). A ruler is counted for each year that he stayed in power. A 100-year moving average is taken to smooth out the excessive fluctuations. The East Asian countries include China, Korea, Japan, and Vietnam.

Figure 13 suggests that the *Keju* system may offer a unique possibility: Monarchies without institutions of credible executive constraint could still achieve political stability. We gather a cross-country panel to empirically investigate the relationship between different institutions (parliament and *Keju*) and political stability. The panel covers 112 historical states spanning the Eurasia continent from the 1st to 18th centuries. The data is collected from multiple sources, including Morby (1989) for ruler information, Blaydes and Chaney (2013) for the timing of parliamentary systems, and Kukhak-Charyowon (1993), Hoan and Khai (1963), Jin et al. (2015) and Chen (2015) for information on *Keju* systems in other East Asian states.[93] The resulting dataset covers 4,119 rulers in 564 dynasties from 112 historical states. We estimate the following model:

$$Stability_{it} = \beta_1 Parliament_{it} + \beta_2 Keju_{it} + \alpha_j + \theta_t + \epsilon_{it}, \tag{3}$$

---

[93] The data on the establishment of *Keju* and the number of *Keju* graduates comes from several sources: *The Complete History of the Imperial Service Examination System in China* (2015), Moongwa Bangmok (1993), and *Dai Viet Lich Trieu Dang Khoa Luc* (1963). The numbers from these books are ultimately based on official government records from the dynasties.

Table 2 The impact of *Keju* on ruler stability

Variables	(1) Ruler duration	(2) Ruler duration	(3) Depose prob.	(4) Depose prob.
Parliament	4.947***	4.786**	−0.0274	−0.0234
	(1.906)	(1.903)	(0.0319)	(0.0319)
*Keju*_dummy	6.044***		−0.146***	
	(1.540)		(0.0528)	
*Keju*_scale		0.141**		−0.00312***
		(0.0281)		(0.000670)
Century and polity FE	Y	Y	Y	Y
Observations	4,058	4,042	2,581	2,565
R-squared	0.191	0.198	0.167	0.174

Note: The unit of analysis is ruler-reign. Robust standard errors are in parentheses. *** indicates $p < 0.01$, ** $p < 0.05$, and * $p < 0.1$. The variable *Keju_Scale* is the average annual number of graduates who passed the *Keju* exams during the ruler's reign.

where i indicates the ruler, t the century, and j the historical polity. The variable *Parliament*$_{it}$ is a dummy taking one if the ruler held at least one parliament meeting during his reign, while *Keju dummy*$_{it}$ takes one if the ruler held at least one Civil Service Examination during his reign. We measure ruler stability with two indicators: the number of years that a ruler stayed in power (*Ruler Duration*) and the annual probability of a ruler being deposed by unnatural means (*Depose Probability*). The results for Equation (3) are provided in Table 2.

Table 2 shows that both parliamentary meetings and *Keju* exams were associated with improved ruler stability. Moreover, Column (1) allows for a direct comparison of the magnitudes of their correlation. The occurrence of parliamentary meetings was associated with a 4.9-year increase in ruler duration, while that of the *Keju* with a 4.8-year increase. The *Keju* system had an even stronger negative correlation with deposition probability than parliament.

The findings presented here suggest the intriguing possibility that the same outcome of political stability could be achieved through diverse institutional solutions. In Western Europe, parliaments offered a venue for peaceful conflict resolution by placing constraints on the monarchs; In East Asia, the establishment of exam-based bureaucratic recruitment could have improved political stability through entirely different channels (discussed in the following subsection). In the Muslim world, neither institution was established, and ruler stability remained relatively low after the medieval period (Blaydes and Chaney, 2013).

5.2 Theoretical Mechanisms

Historians have long recognized the importance of *Keju* for the stability and coherence of dynastic rules in China. In Elman's words, the *Keju* system "was the sine qua non for gentry officials and aristocratic rulers to maintain their proper balance and direction between each other and vis-a-vis the society at large" (Elman, 2013).

This subsection discusses several theoretical mechanisms that might explain the link between *Keju* and political stability. Here, the literature is vast and multidisciplinary. Our survey is by no means exhaustive.

5.2.1 Elite Politics

There has been an extensive debate over the meritocratic nature of the exam system (see Section 5.2.4). Leaving that debate aside, it is important to note that a system does not need to achieve perfect meritocracy to enhance political stability. As long as *Keju* improved social mobility to some extent, it would allow a broader segment of society to be considered for office, ultimately benefiting the ruler. This idea is rooted in the selectorate theory pioneered by De Mesquita et al. (2005), which argues that rulers rely on a core group of supporters (the "winning coalition") drawn from a larger pool of political insiders known as the "selectorate." A ruler's political survival is most secure when the selectorate is much larger than the winning coalition, as the ruler can easily replace members of the winning coalition with others from the selectorate, drawing on a larger base of support.

In the Chinese context, the bureaucracy, or its upper echelon consisting of the top political elites, can be thought of as the winning coalition. The exam system expanded the size of the selectorate by opening up bureaucratic eligibility to more individuals, particularly from the lower elites, reducing the importance of birth, family prestige, and other restrictive factors for office. As the selectorate grew larger, individual members became more interchangeable, giving the ruler greater control and reducing the bargaining power of any particular family or group within the top political elite.

There is a rich historical literature on the importance of *Keju* in China's transition away from an age dominated by the aristocracy (e.g. Bol, 1992;

Lu, 2016), recently further validated by the empirical work of Wen, Wang, and Hout (2024) and in Section 3. Huang and Yang (2022) were among the first to propose an explanation of *Keju*'s stability implication based on a formal political theory. Our empirical results in Section 4 also collaborate with this argument. The exam system indeed broadened political access to a much larger population and limited the impact of birth and family.

5.2.2 Popular Support

Scholars have long underscored how the exam system facilitated an impressive degree of social mobility within the confines of a premodern society (e.g. Ho, 1962; Chaffee, 1995; Elman, 2013). This prospect for upward advancement, albeit modest, offered people an avenue to pursue personal aspirations without disrupting the *ancien régime*. Crucially, it elevated the opportunity cost of rebellion against the ruler.

This mechanism applied particularly well to the Chinese gentry, the elite group that benefited most from the exam system. However, its impact extended beyond the elite to broader society. Although immediate success in the exams and entry into elite circles was difficult for the lower classes, who made up the majority of society, the system offered the hope of eventual social mobility through the accumulation of wealth and educational resources over generations (Elman, 2013). The prospect that their sons and grandsons could attain such status likely fostered a pacifying attitude toward the regime among the lower classes, encouraging them to focus on improving their own well-being through legal means and reducing potential dissent.

Empirically, Bai and Jia (2016) show that the abrupt termination of the exam system in 1905 directly contributed to popular uprisings against the dynastic regime in the early 20th century. With avenues of social mobility now closed, those would-be elites resorted to revolution against the regime. Liu (2023) argues that meritocracy can be used to co-opt large numbers of ordinary citizens by providing them with an opportunity of socioeconomic advancement in lieu of income redistribution (which is theoretically seen as detrimental to the interest of autocrats), as long as the selection process is viewed as inclusive and rule-based. Even though Liu (2023) focuses on civil service examinations in contemporary China, the same mechanism would have worked in a historical setting as well. On the negative side, Kuipers (2023) shows that failing the civil service exam can decrease applicants' belief in the legitimacy of the process and levels of national identification, relying on the contemporary example of Indonesia.

5.2.3 Regional Representation

In 1397, in one of the first *Keju* exams ever administered for the new Ming dynasty, the founding emperor was furious to find all fifty-one candidates who passed the palace exam that year coming from the southern provinces of China. Following an extensive investigation, he ordered the execution of several high-ranking court officials and banished numerous others. He personally reviewed all the exam papers and selected an additional sixty-one candidates, this time all from the north (Hucker, 2008).

At the time, the southern regions of China boasted considerably higher levels of development than the north. To the extent that wealth could readily translate into educational investment and human capital, it is reasonable to expect better exam performance from southern candidates. To complicate the matter further, the founding emperor of the Ming dynasty, as well as the great majority of his generals, were originally from the south. The south had contributed significantly more resources and manpower to his earlier military campaigns. If a ruler's primary concern was to reward loyal followers, the logical course for the founding emperor should be to prioritize exam candidates from the south.

Yet, rather remarkably, he chose to extend political benefits to groups that hadn't played a direct role in his ascent to power. This deliberate choice was probably rooted in his belief that, for his government to garner widespread support, it was imperative to encompass members from all regions.

Section 4 already highlighted how the elimination of the centralized elite by war in the late 9th and early 10th centuries inadvertently allowed future rulers to enforce regional quotas more strictly. Since the Song dynasty, candidates from all regions of China were admitted to the final stages of the exam, where they competed for *Jinshi* degrees and the final rankings. However, due to the ongoing North versus South controversy, further reforms were deemed necessary: not only should the body of contestants reflect regional diversity, but also the final winners. Under the Ming, a quota system was introduced at the highest level (for the *Jinshi* holders) – dividing China into northern, southern, and central regions.[94] The later Qing dynasty further refined this quota structure in a way that allowed the emperors to easily adjust the regional composition of governmental personnel.

Political representation lies at the core of modern democratic politics. In democratic regimes, a representative pursues the interest of the people who

---

[94] These quotas roughly mirrored population distribution, but they had a populist appeal: They further disadvantaged the southeastern region of China, which had the empire's strongest scholastic tradition (Hucker, 2008).

have the right to elect her. However, Rehfeld (2006) argues that political representation does not have to be a democratic phenomenon at all. Political representation could also arise in nondemocratic settings.

Strictly speaking, the regional representation within the *Keju* didn't align precisely with modern concepts of political representation. Rather, it functioned as a mechanism for the emperor to distribute political rents and allocate power strategically. Nonetheless, to the extent that the interests of officials might partially overlap with those of their native regions, their presence in the central government could also serve to advance the interests of their hometowns. In this light, *Keju* might be viewed as an example of a premodern, nondemocratic form of political representation. Xue and Zhang (2021) show that a provincial quota system reform initiated in 1712 expanded opportunities for individuals from underrepresented provinces and mitigated cross-provincial inequality in political access. Chen, Kung, and Ma (2020) document a wide range of positive impacts that the *Keju* had on local communities, including better educational infrastructure, a higher level of social capital, and a culture that valued education. Thus, the exam system likely contributed to political stability by enhancing regional representation within the imperial government and facilitating greater inclusion across provinces. Another mechanism linking regional representation to political stability is that a geographically diverse body of government officials also makes it difficult for elite coordination and collusion against the ruler.[95]

5.2.4 The Debate on Meritocracy

An intellectual tradition in the English literature that traces back to Enlightenment thinkers, such as Voltaire and Quesnay, and later Weber, considered the *Keju* system a form of meritocratic governance. Many China scholars, coming from entirely different traditions, also view *Keju* as, at least, relatively meritocratic for a premodern institution (e.g. Elman, 2013; Chen, Kung, and Ma, 2020; Huang, 2023). However, the exact definition of meritocracy seems to vary across individuals and disciplines. While some scholars regard it a critical feature of meritocracy to provide equal opportunities for all social groups, others emphasize that meritocracy is a system that rewards competence and effort. Often, studies do not explicitly distinguish the two definitions as it is implied that one would naturally lead to another.

The literature continues to engage in debates regarding the extent of *Keju*'s meritocratic nature due to at least two unresolved issues. Regarding the first

---

[95] This is particularly true when officials from such diverse regional backgrounds do not intermarry with one another. See Wang (2022).

definition of meritocracy as equalizing opportunities, opponents highlight the enduring advantage wielded by affluent families and political insiders within the *Keju* system (Huang, 2016b; Paik, Hong, and Yun, 2022; Peng, 2023).[96] Regarding the second definition emphasizing competence selection, opponents point to a wide gap between the necessary skill set required for a government job – arguably, administrative capacity and statecraft – and the actual content of the exams, which primarily focused on a formulaic, politically correct understanding of Confucian classics (Bai, 2019; Huang, 2023; Peng, 2023, but see Kung, Liu, and Zhang, 2025).

However, the literature overlooks a crucial third aspect: a potential trade-off between equalizing opportunity and competence-based selection. The extent of this trade-off hinges on the natural distribution of talent within the population. Should innate talent be randomly distributed across various social groups, a competence-based system automatically necessitates equalizing opportunities. On the other hand, if family backgrounds affect personal competence via the bequeath of cultural capital and political know-how, a genuinely competence-based "meritocratic" system might still reflect a certain level of insider advantage and wealth effect. From this perspective, determining the meritocratic nature of *Keju* entails the formidable empirical task of gauging the output of the exam system against the underlying "competence distribution" in the population, which is beyond the scope of our Element.

Nonetheless, it is worth noting that all three political mechanisms discussed from Section 5.2.1 to 5.2.3 require equalizing opportunity, but not necessarily competence-based meritocracy. Combining with competence-based meritocracy would certainly amplify the impact, but even if mobility was engineered by random reshuffling of social status, it would have an impact on political stability as well. In other words, equalizing opportunity can be more important than competence-based meritocracy from the perspective of political stability.

This equalizing consideration could explain why the exam curriculum became narrower and more stringent over time, as a limited curriculum emphasizing memorization would help minimize the advantage of family background. A related argument can also be made to explain why the Qing dynasty rulers failed to incorporate modern scientific studies into the *Keju* curriculum when calls for modernization were on the rise as China suffered military defeats and

---

[96] In the context of our discussion, which explores the potential influence of the *Keju* on political stability, this objection may not entirely discredit the meritocracy argument, as long as the exam system represented a relatively *more* "meritocratic" approach compared to preceding institutions, such as hereditary succession, *Chaju*, and the NRRS. Statistical evidence in Sections 3 and especially 4 also highlights the limits of family background as a predictor of exam success.

territorial encroachments by Western powers in the 19th century. An exam testing candidates on modern science would primarily benefit elite families, especially the already wealthy ones from southeastern regions of China that had enjoyed high exposure to the West since the mid-19th century, and thus diminish *Keju*'s equalizing effect. We have no direct evidence to prove whether the Chinese monarchs were acutely aware of this trade-off. Still, many of their policies throughout history constantly reflected efforts to navigate the trade-off between equality and competence. Sections 3 and 4 detailed numerous procedures adopted by the imperial governments to preserve the equalizing potential of the exams, such as affirmative action policies that discriminated against the *Zidi* in the Tang, anonymization and transcription of the exam paper in the Song, regional quota at various levels in the Ming and Qing sometimes even at the expense of regions with great human capital, and the establishment of publicly funded schools throughout the second millennium. Many such reforms were initiated under the name of "meritocracy." Even though their impact on personal competence might be debatable,[97] they all effectively promoted equal opportunity.

5.3 Conclusion

This section explores the potential influence of the exam system on political stability. To contextualize our discussion, we start with a cross-country panel regression based on 112 historical states. Our findings reveal a positive correlation between the adoption of the exam system and ruler stability. Notably, the significance of this correlation rivals the impact observed for the establishment of parliamentary systems in Europe. To establish theoretical underpinnings, we propose three potential mechanisms that explain the connection between the *Keju* system and political stability. Finally, to conclude this section, we engage in a discussion regarding the definition and implications of meritocracy within the context of political stability.

It is worth emphasizing that *Keju* was not the only path to autocratic stability in general or the sole reason for monarchical supremacy in China. The Chinese state was already moving toward recentralization before the establishment of *Keju* (e.g. Chen, Wang, and Zhang, 2025). Sections 2 and 3 underscore the gradual and concurrent institutionalization of the exam system alongside

---

[97] For example, Elman (2013) noticed that public dynastic schools became testing centers with limited educational function by the late imperial period. For regional quota, our finding in Section 3 shows that candidates from wealthy areas continued to score high in the national exams even after the quota imposed by the central government limited the total number of candidates from these areas. This could suggest a genuinely higher level of human capital from these wealthy regions, which the central government chose to limit.

other political developments that could also influence political stability. Additionally, Chinese rulers since the 9th century likely recognized the political implications of *Keju* and deliberately promoted the system alongside other measures to reinforce imperial power. Section 2.2.6 already highlights the futility of quantitatively identifying the "causal effect" of the *Keju* treatment. The mixed-methods approach in this Element is better suited for the question at hand, and the more plausible verdict is that *Keju* made an already powerful monarchy even more so.

Lastly, another issue often associated with *Keju* is Confucianism. This ideology was central to the *Keju* system and exam materials and was promoted alongside the exam apparatus for millennia. It validated state authority and advocated loyalty to the ruler as the highest moral conduct dedicated to state welfare. Confucianism's influence on China's political development and stability is well-documented, and *Keju* likely contributed to its indoctrination. Due to space constraints and the extensive literature on this topic, we do not elaborate further (see Elman (2000) and Zhao (2015) for more details).

References

Bai, Ying. 2019. "Farewell to Confucianism: The modernizing effect of dismantling China's imperial examination system." *Journal of Development Economics* 141:102382.

Bai, Ying and Ruixue Jia. 2016. "Elite recruitment and political stability: The impact of the abolition of China's civil service exam." *Econometrica* 84(2):677–733.

Bielenstein, Hans. 1986. *The institutions of Later Han.* Vol. 1 of *The Cambridge History of China.* Cambridge University Press, pp. 491–519.

Blaydes, Lisa and Eric Chaney. 2013. "The feudal revolution and Europe's rise: Political divergence of the Christian west and the Muslim world before 1500 CE." *American Political Science Review* 107(1):16–34.

Bol, Peter. 1992. *"This culture of ours": Intellectual transitions in T'ang and Sung China.* Stanford University Press.

Boucoyannis, Deborah. 2021. *Kings as judges: Power, justice, and the origins of parliaments.* Cambridge University Press.

Brown, Miranda and Yu Xie. 2015. "Between heaven and earth: Dual accountability in Han China." *Chinese Journal of Sociology* 1(1):56–87.

Campbell, Cameron and James Lee. 2003. "Social mobility from a kinship perspective: Rural Liaoning, 1789–1909." *International Review of Social History* 48(1):1–26.

Cen, Zhongmian. 2020. *Sui Tang Shi (History of the Sui-Tang Dynasties).* Shanghai Guji Chuban She (Shanghai Classics Publishing House).

Chaffee, John. 1995. *The The thorny gates of learning in Sung China.* State University of New York Press.

Chen, Joy and Erik H. Wang. 2024. "State-building or State-weakening? The consequences of military control in medieval China." *Working Paper.*

Chen, Joy, Erik H. Wang, and Xiaoming Zhang. 2024. "From powerholders to stakeholders: State-building with elite compensation in early medieval China." *American Journal of Political Science* 1–17. **URL:** https://onlinelibrary.wiley.com/doi/abs/10.1111/ajps.12888.

Chen, Shuo, Xinyu Fan, and Zhichen Huang. 2023. "Noble no more: Keju, checks and balances, and political purges." *Working Paper, Available at SSRN: http://dx.doi.org/10.2139/ssrn.4523770 (access date: December 12, 2023).*

Chen, Song. 2017. "The state, the gentry, and local institutions: The Song dynasty and long-term trends from Tang to Qing." *Journal of Chinese History* 中國歷史學刊 1(1):141–182.

Chen, Ting. and James K. Kung. 2019. "Why Song China? The rise of a merchant class and the emergence of meritocracy." *Working Paper*.

Chen, Ting, James Kai-sing Kung, and Chicheng Ma. 2020. "Long live Keju! The persistent effects of China's civil examination system." *The Economic Journal* 130(631):2030–2064.

Chen, Wen. 2015. Research on the Vietnamese Imperial Examination System. Beijing: The Commercial Press.

Chen, Yinke. 1982. *Tangdai Zhengzhi Shi Shulungao*. Shanghai Guji Chubanshe.

Cheng, Cheng, David Stasavage, and Yuhua Wang. 2023. "The written word and the development of the state in China and Europe." *Working Paper*.

Cox, Gary W. 2017. "Political institutions, economic liberty, and the great divergence." *The Journal of Economic History* 77(3):724–755.

Dalby, Michael T. 1979. *Court politics in late T'ang times*. The Cambridge History of China. Cambridge University Press, pp. 561–681.

De Mesquita, Bruce Bueno, Alastair Smith, Randolph M. Siverson, and James D. Morrow. 2005. *The logic of political survival*. MIT press.

Dincecco, Mark. 2017. *State capacity and economic development: Present and past*. Cambridge University Press.

Dincecco, Mark and Yuhua Wang. 2018. "Violent conflict and political development over the long run: China versus Europe." *Annual Review of Political Science* 21(1):341–358.

Doran, Rebecca. 2017. 95Education and the examination system. In Denecke, Wiebke, Wai-yee Li, and Xiaofei Tian, eds., *The Oxford Handbook of Classical Chinese Literature* (1000 BCE-900 CE). Oxford University Press. **URL:** https://doi.org/10.1093/oxfordhb/9780199356591.013.7.

Downing, Brian. 1992. *The military revolution and political change: Origins of democracy and autocracy in early modern Europe*. Princeton University Press.

Ebrey, Patricia Buckley. 1978. *The Aristocratic families in early imperial China: A case study of the Po-Ling Tsui family*. Cambridge University Press.

Elman, Benjamin. 2000. *A cultural history of civil service exam in late imperial China*. University of California Press.

Elman, Benjamin A. 2013. *Civil examinations and meritocracy in late imperial China*. Harvard University Press.

Fan, Zhaofei. 2014. *Zhonggu Taiyuan Shizu Qunti Yanjiu (The group of Taiyuan Aristocratic families in medieval China)*. Zhonghua Book.

Fernández-Villaverde, Jesús, Mark Koyama, Youhong Lin, and Tuan-Hwee Sng. 2023. "The fractured-land hypothesis." *The Quarterly Journal of Economics* 138(2):1173–1231.

Fu, Xuancong. 2020. *Tangdai Keju yu Wenxue (Imperial examination system and literature in the Tang)*. Zhonghua Book (Zhonghua shuju).

Fu, Xuancong. 2023. *Li Deyu Nianpu (The chronology of Li Deyu)*. Zhonghua Book (Zhonghua shuju).

Guo, Chao. 2019. "Lun Beizhou Zhongzheng de Fazhan yu Yanbian (The development of the 'Jiu Pin Zhong Zheng' system at the Northern Zhou Dynasty)." *Weijin Nanbeichao Suitang Shi Ziliao (Journal of the 3–9th Century Chinese History)* 40:136–162.

Hartwell, Robert M. 1982. "Demographic, political, and social transformations of China, 750–1550." *Harvard Journal of Asiatic Studies* 42(2):365–442.

He, Zhongli. 2000. "Ershi Shiji de Zhongguo Keju Zhidu Shi Yanjiu (Research in the 20th century on the history of Keju as an institution)." *Lishi Yanjiu (Historical Research)* 6:146–149.

Ho, Ping-ti. 1962. *The Ladder of Success in Imperial China: Aspects of social mobility, 1368–1911*. Columbia University Press.

Hoan, Nguyen and Ta Thuc Khai. 1963. The Register of Successful Candidates in the Dynastic Examinations of Đại Việt. Hanoi: Ministry of Education.

Hout, Michael. 2012. "Social and economic returns to higher education in the United States." *Annual Review of Sociology* 38:379–400.

Huang, Ray. 1996. *China: A macro history*. Routledge.

Huang, Shoucheng. 2014. "Beizhou Zhengquan Shifou Shixingle Jiupin Zhongzhengzhi? (Did the northern Zhou Regime implement the nine-rank rectifying system?)." *Wen Shi Zhe (Literature, History, and Philosophy)* 343:97–115.

Huang, Shoucheng. 2016*a*. "Beizhou Zhengquan Chaju Zhidu Kaoshi (On the Chaju system in northern Zhou)." *Beijing Shifan Daxue Xuebao, Shehui Kexue Ban (Beijing Normal University Proceedings (Social Sciences))* 257:106–115.

Huang, Yasheng. 2023. *The rise and fall of the EAST: How exams, autocracy, stability, and technology brought China success, and why they might lead to its decline*. Yale University Press.

Huang, Yasheng and Clair Yang. 2022. "A longevity mechanism of Chinese absolutism." *The Journal of Politics* 84(2):1165–1175.

Huang, Yifei. 2016*b*. Essays in economic history and applied microeconomics. PhD thesis California Institute of Technology.

Hucker, Charles. 2008. Ming government. In Mote, Frederick W., and Denis C. Twitchett, eds., *The Cambridge history of China, Vol 8: The Ming dynasty part II*, 1368-1644. Cambridge University Press.

Hymes, Robert P. 1986. *Statesmen and gentlemen: The elite of Fu-chou, Chiang-hsi, in northern and southern Sung*. Cambridge University Press.

Imai, Kosuke, Luke Keele, Dustin Tingley, and Teppei Yamamoto. 2011. "Unpacking the black box of causality: Learning about causal mechanisms from experimental and observational studies." *American Political Science Review* 105(4):765–789.

Jia, Ruixue, Gérard Roland, and Yang Xie. 2023. "A theory of power structure and institutional compatibility: China vs. Europe revisited." *Journal of the European Economic Association*, Volume 22, Issue 3, June 2024, pp. 1275-1318, p. jvad050.

Jiang, Aihua. 2006. "Tang ren shou ming shui ping ji si wang yuan yin shi tan tao – yi mu zhi zi liao wei zhong xin (An exploration of the life expectancy and causes of death of Tang Dynasty people: Focusing on epitaphs)." *Zhongguo shi yan jiu (Studies in Chinese History)* 2006(4):59–76.

Jiang, Aihua. 2012. "Tang dai zhong xia ceng guan yuan ru shi zhi lu yan jiu – yi mu zhi ming zi liao wei zhong xin (A study of the path of entry into officialdom for middle- and lower-level officials in the Tang Dynasty: Focusing on epitaphs)." *Qianyan (Frontier)* 23:16–19.

Jin, Yingkun. 2015. *Zhongguo ke ju zhi du tong shi: Sui Tang wu dai juan (A comprehensive history of the Chinese imperial examination system: The Sui, Tang, and Five Dynasties periods)*. Shanghai ren min chu ban she (Shanghai People's Publishing House).

Jin, Yingkun, Xiqing Zhang, Yuhuan Wu, et al. 2015. *The complete history of civil service examination system in China, 1st Edition*. Shanghai People's Publishing House.

Kuipers, Nicholas. 2023. "Failing the test: The countervailing attitudinal effects of civil service examinations." *American Political Science Review* 117(3):891–908.

Kukhak Charyowon. Moongwa Bangmok. 1993. *Sama Pangmok*. Kookhak Institute.

Kung, James Kai-sing. 2022. "On the origins and persistent effects of the world's first meritocratic institution." *Comparative Economic Studies* 64(4):563–581.

Kung, James, Kevin Zhengcheng Liu, and Xiaoming Zhang. 2025. "Merit-based recruitment and government performance: Evidence from random assignment of administrators." *Working Paper*.

Lai, Ruihe. 2008. *Tangdai Jiceng Wenguan (Lower-ranked civilian officials in the Tang)*. Zhonghua Book (Zhonghua shuju).

Lai, Ruihe. 2011. *Tangdai Zhongceng Wenguan (Mid-ranked civilian officials in the Tang)*. Zhonghua Book (Zhonghua shuju).

Leventoğlu, Bahar. 2005. "Social mobility and political transitions." *Journal of Theoretical Politics* 17(4):465–496.

Liu, Haifeng. 2000. "Keju Zhi de Qiyuan Yu Jinshike de Kaishi (The origins of Keju and the beginning of the Jinshi exam category)." *Li shi yan jiu (Historical Research)* 6:3–16.

Liu, Hanzhang. 2023. "Meritocracy as authoritarian co-optation: Political selection and upward mobility in China." *Working Paper. Available at SSRN 4567133.*

Lou, Jin. 2019. "Tracing the origin of the practice of "self-recommendation by submitting papers' (Toudie Ziju) in the imperial examination system (Keju Zhi Toudie Ziju Zhifa Suyuan)." *Historical Research (Lishi Yanjiu)* 1:55–72.

Lu, Yang. 2016. *Qingliu Wenhua Yu Tang Diguo*. Beijing Daxue Chuban She.

Maddicott, John. 2015. "Magna Carta and the origins of parliament." *Historian* 125:22.

Mahoney, James, and Kathleen Thelen, 2009. "A theory of gradual institutional change." In Mahoney, James, and Kathleen Thelen, eds., *Explaining Institutional Change: Ambiguity, Agency, and Power* 1:1. Cambridge University Press

Mao, Hanguang. 1988. *Zhongguo Zhonggu Shehui Shilun (Historical research on medieval Chinese society)*. Linking.

McMullen, David. 1988. *State and scholars in T'ang China*. Cambridge University Press.

Miyazaki, Ichisada. 1977. *Kyuhin kanjinho no kenku: Kakyo zenshi (Studies of the regulations of the nine ranks bureaucratic system: The prehistory of the examination system)*. Dobosha.

Miyazaki, Ichisada. 1981. *China's examination hell: The civil service examinations of imperial China*. Yale University Press.

Morby, John. 1989. *Dynasties of the world: A chronological and genealogical handbook*. Oxford University Press.

North, Douglass C. and Barry R. Weingast. 1989. "Constitutions and commitment: The evolution of institutions governing public choice in seventeenth-century England." *The Journal of Economic History* 49(4):803–832.

Paik, Christopher, Sok Chul Hong, and Yangkeun Yun. 2022. "The road to ascension: Exams, lineages and civil servants of the Joseon Dynasty." *Working Paper*.

Peng, Peng. 2023. "Examination as socialization: Unravel the myth of meritocracy in China." *Working Paper*.

Pierson, Paul. 2004. "Politics in time: History, institutions, and social analysis." Princeton University Press.

Qiu, Luming. 2016. "Zhi zuo jun wang: Zhonggu Zhongguo nan yang zhang shi de xing cheng (Making local prestige: The formation of the Zhang lineage in Nanyang during the medieval period)." *Li shi yan jiu (Historical Research)* 3:21–39.

Qiu, Luming. 2018. *Changan Yu Hebei Zhijian: Zhongwan Tang De Zhengzhi Yu Wenhua (Between Changan and Hebei: The politics and culture of the mid-to-late Tang)*. Beijing Shifan Daxue Chubanshe.

Rehfeld, Andrew. 2006. "Towards a general theory of political representation." *The Journal of Politics* 68(1):1–21.

Shiue, Carol H. 2016. Social mobility in the long run: An analysis with five linked generations in China, 1300–1900. Technical report. *Working paper*.

Stasavage, David. 2003. *Public debt and the Birth of the democratic state: France and Great Britain 1688–1789*. Cambridge University Press.

Stasavage, David. 2020. *The decline and rise of democracy: A global history from antiquity to today*. Princeton University Press.

Strayer, Joseph R. 1970. *On the medieval origins of the modern state*. Princeton University Press.

Sun, Guodong. 1980. *On the history and Tang and Song Dynasties (Tang Song Lishi Luncong)*. Shanghai Classics Publishing House.

Tackett, Nicolas. 2014. *The destruction of the medieval Chinese aristocracy*. Harvard University Asia Center.

Tackett, Nicolas. 2020. "The evolution of the Tang political elite and its marriage network." *Journal of Chinese History* 4(2):277–304.

Tang, Changru. 2010. *Weijin Nanbeichao Shi Luncong (Collection of essays on the Wei-Jin and north and south dynasties)*. Shangwu Yinshu Guan (Commercial Press).

The National Atlas Compilation Committee. 2012. *The Historical Atlas of People's Republic of China*. Cartographic Publishing House of China, China Social Science Press.

Torche, Florencia. 2011. "Is a college degree still the great equalizer? Intergenerational mobility across levels of schooling in the United States." *American Journal of Sociology* 117(3):763–807.

Wagner, Donald B. 2001. *The state and the iron industry in Han China*. Vol. 44. NIAS Press.

Wang, Erik H. 2024. "Dingliang ShehuiKexue Nengwei LishiXue Dailai Shenme? Yi ZhongguShizu Weili (What can quantitative social science bring to the study of history? The case of the medieval Chinese Aristocracy)." *Xueshu Yuekan (Academic Monthly)* 56(6):128–130.

Wang, Yanping. 2018. *Niu Li Dangzheng Kaolun (A study on the Niu-Li factional strife)*. Sichuan Renmin Chubanshe (Sichuan People's Press).

Wang, Yuhua. 2022. *The rise and fall of imperial China: The social origins of state development*. Vol. 17. Princeton University Press.

Wang, Zhenglu. 1995. *Weijin Nanbeichao Guanliao Tizhi Yanjiu (Research on the bureaucracy in the Wei-Jin and north and south dynasties)*. Fujian Renmin Chuban She (Fujian People's Press).

Wen, Fangqi, Erik H. Wang, and Michael Hout. 2024. "Social mobility in the Tang Dynasty as the imperial examination rose and aristocratic family pedigree declined, 618–907 CE." *Proceedings of the National Academy of Sciences* 121(4):e2305564121. **URL:** www.pnas.org/doi/abs/10.1073/pnas.2305564121.

Wu, Zongguo. 1992. *tangdai keju zhidu yanjiu (A study of the imperial examination in Tang Dynasty)*. Liaoning University Press.

Xiang, Niandong. 2012. "Cen Zhongmian's Critique of Chen Yinke and His Own Issues (Cen Zhongmian Dui Chen Yinke De Xueshu Piping Jiqi Neizai Wenti)." *Tribune of Social Sciences (Shehui Kexu Luntan)* (3):159–184.

Xue, Melanie Meng and Boxiao Zhang. 2021. "The short-and long-run effects of affirmative action: Evidence from imperial China." *Available at SSRN 3997918*.

Yan, Buke. 2017. *Bofeng Yu Bogu: Qinhan Weijin Nanbeichao De Zhengzhi Wenming (Crests and troughs: Politics of Qin, Han, Wei, Jin and northern and southern dynasties)*. Beijing Daxue Chubanshe.

Yan, Buke. 2021. *Chaju Zhidu Bianqian Shigao (Historical research on political selection and recruitment)*. Beijing Shifan Daxue Chubanshe.

Yanming, Gong and Zu Hui. 2014. *Comprehensive records of the imperial examination in the Song Dynasty*. 1st ed. Guangxi Normal University Press.

Zhang, Lawrence. 2022. *Power for a price: The purchase of official appointments in Qing China*. Harvard University Asia Center.

Zhang, Xuhua. 2015. *Jiupin Zhongzhengzhi Yanjiu (A study of the nine-rank system)*. Zhonghua Shuju.

Zhao, Dingxin. 2015. *The Confucian-legalist state: A new theory of Chinese history*. Oxford University Press.

Acknowledgments

The authors thank Iza Ding, Patricia Ebrey, Pierre Landry, Xiaobo Lü, Xiao Ma, and Ashutosh Varshney, as well as the participants at the 2023 American Political Science Association Annual Meeting, the 2023 Symposium on Comprehensive Modernization and Political Development at Zhejiang University, and the 2024 Deep Roots Conference at the Complexity Science Hub Vienna, for their thoughtful feedback. We are deeply grateful to Cameron Campbell for his helpful advice on data. We also greatly appreciate the comments and support from David Stasavage, Mark Dincecco, and an anonymous referee, which have been invaluable in shaping the development of this work. Finally, we are thankful to Ao Ge, Yuying Jiang, Lulu Li, Sunny Junyang Li, Jiahui Xu, and Yunzhong Zhang for their superb research assistance.

Cambridge Elements

Political Economy

Mark Dincecco
University of Michigan

Mark Dincecco is Professor of Political Science at the University of Michigan. His research analyzes the long-run historical determinants of the political and economic development patterns that we observe today, with a focus on Europe and Eurasia. Dincecco has published numerous articles in leading academic journals across both political science and economics. His most recent book is From *Warfare to Wealth: The Military Origins of Urban Prosperity in Europe*, the winner of the William Riker Best Book Award. Dincecco received his PhD in Economics from UCLA.

About the Series

The Element Series Political Economy provides authoritative contributions on important topics in the rapidly growing field of political economy. Elements are designed so as to provide broad and in-depth coverage combined with original insights from scholars in political science, economics, and economic history. Contributions are welcome on any topic within this field.

Cambridge Elements

Political Economy

Elements in the Series

Lynching and Local Justice: Legitimacy and Accountability in Weak States
Danielle F. Jung and Dara Kay Cohen

The Economic Origin of Political Parties
Christopher Kam and Adlai Newson

Backsliding: Democratic Regress in the Contemporary World
Stephan Haggard and Robert Kaufman

A Moral Political Economy: Present, Past, and Future
Federica Carugati and Margaret Levi

One Road to Riches?: How State Building and Democratization Affect Economic Development
Haakon Gjerløw, Carl Henrik Knutsen, Tore Wig and Matthew Charles Wilson

Geography, Capacity, and Inequality: Spatial Inequality
Pablo Beramendi and Melissa Rogers

Democratization and the State: Competence, Control, and Performance in Indonesia's Civil Service
Jan Henryk Pierskalla

Reforming to Survive: The Bolshevik Origins of Social Policies
Magnus B. Rasmussen and Carl Henrik Knutsen

The Puzzle of Clientelism: Political Discretion and Elections Around the World
Miriam A. Golden and Eugenia Nazrullaeva

Representation and Taxation in the American South, 1820–1910
Jeffrey Jensen, Giuliana Pardelli and Jeffrey F. Timmons

Democracy in Trouble: Democratic Resilience and Breakdown from 1900 to 2022
Myles Williamson, Christopher Akor and Amanda B. Edgell

The Political Economy of China's Imperial Examination System
Erik H. Wang and Clair Z. Yang

A full series listing is available at: www.cambridge.org/EPEC

For EU product safety concerns, contact us at Calle de José Abascal, 56–1°, 28003 Madrid, Spain or eugpsr@cambridge.org.

www.ingramcontent.com/pod-product-compliance
Ingram Content Group UK Ltd.
Pitfield, Milton Keynes, MK11 3LW, UK
UKHW021831200625
459904UK00016B/235